MOSAICS : practical projects for the home

MOSAICS : practical projects for the home

Stylish ideas and easy-to-follow techniques with over 25 step-by-step decorative designs and over 350 photographs

HELEN BAIRD

southwater

This edition is published by Southwater

Southwater is an imprint of Anness Publishing Ltd
Hermes House, 88–89 Blackfriars Road, London SE1 8HA
tel. 020 7401 2077; fax 020 7633 9499
www.southwaterbooks.com; info@anness.com

UK agent: The Manning Partnership Ltd, 6 The Old Dairy, Melcombe Road, Bath BA2 3LR;
tel. 01225 478444; fax 01225 478440; sales@manning-partnership.co.uk

UK distributor: Grantham Book Services Ltd, Isaac Newton Way, Alma Park Industrial Estate,
Grantham, Lincs NG31 9SD; tel. 01476 541080; fax 01476 541061; orders@gbs.tbs-ltd.co.uk

North American agent/distributor: National Book Network, 4501 Forbes Boulevard,
Suite 200, Lanham, MD 20706; tel. 301 459 3366; fax 301 429 5746; www.nbnbooks.com

Australian agent/distributor: Pan Macmillan Australia, Level 18, St Martins Tower,
31 Market St, Sydney, NSW 2000; tel. 1300 135 113; fax 1300 135 103;
customer.service@macmillan.com.au

New Zealand agent/distributor: David Bateman Ltd, 30 Tarndale Grove, Off Bush Road,
Albany, Auckland; tel. (09) 415 7664; fax (09) 415 8892

A CIP catalogue record for this book is available from the British Library.

Publisher   Joanna Lorenz
Editorial Director   Judith Simons
Project Editors   Doreen Gillon and Katy Bevan
Designer   Adelle Morris
Production Controller   Claire Rae
Additional text   Marion Elliot, Celia Gregory, Mary Maguire, Cleo Mussi and Caroline Suter
Photography   Polly Eltes, Rodney Forte, Tim Imrie, Zul Mukhida, Debbie Patterson,
    Spike Powell, Adrian Taylor and Debbi Treloar

Previously published as part of a larger volume, *Mosaics by Design*

10 9 8 7 6 5 4 3 2 1

Publisher's note
Projects are graded for difficulty from 1–5 indicated by this brush symbol.

The author and the publisher have made every effort to ensure that all the instructions
contained in this book are accurate and that the safest methods are recommended.
Readers should follow all recommended safety procedures and wear protective
goggles, gloves and clothing at all times during the making of mosaics. You should
know how to use all your tools and equipment safely and make sure you are
confident about what you are doing. The publisher and author cannot accept
liability for any injury, damage or loss to persons or property as a result of using
any equipment in this book or carrying out any of the projects.

Contents

Modern mosaicists work in all manner of styles and bring immense flair to the art. Some draw on traditional influences and methods, while others forge new ground in their use of scale, form and materials.

Introduction

There has been a renewed interest in mosaic among the general public, and mosaic is now being applied to all kinds of objects in the decorative arts and sculpture, for private enjoyment, and to decorate public places. You can see the effectiveness of mosaic as a hard-wearing design element in locations as varied as railway stations, swimming pools, cafés, bars and shopping centres, as well as private homes.

Mosaic artists all around the world derive inspiration from many sources, including nature, animal and plant forms, and the human form, as well as from the repeating or geometric patterns typical of Greek, Roman, Celtic and Cubist art. Some artists employ traditional materials in exciting new ways, and others incorporate more unusual materials and textures in their work. Follow their initiative and experiment with mosaic, as there are few rules about combining traditional materials such as smalti with more innovative materials in the projects you choose to make for your home. You can quickly develop your own motifs, style and colourways. Just make sure that the mosaic is waterproof where necessary, such as in a bathroom, or level where it needs to be, such as on a floor.

The choice of projects is vast. You can decorate interiors with small portable panels and accessories to begin with, and once you are more confident, aim for larger expanses of wall, and floors, as well as decorative sculptures.

Above: This freestanding sculpture is a funky, brightly coloured guitar by mosaic artist Elizabeth De'Ath.

Left: Mosaic is an applied art that can complement contemporary interiors. This modern-looking mirror frame was worked out on paper first, before the final design was settled on.

Opposite: A pyramid sculpture created with chicken wire and cement by artist Celia Gregory. The mosaic is made from small pieces of rectangular mirror and stained glass.

The wide choice of materials available means that designing a mosaic is a highly personal process. You need to consider such aspects as size, location, function and colour before starting work.

Practicalities

Above: Square tiles are the basis of most mosaic work and can be laid whole or clipped into tesserae of the desired shape and laid in a variety of ways.

Left: Fairies – *a beautiful abstract image of three fairies made from mirror and iridescent stained glass by Celia Gregory.*

When you are designing with mosaic, you have the liberty to use just one material, such as smalti, or to combine as many as you wish. Sometimes, this freedom can make it harder to reach decisions. Of course, no object exists in a vacuum and there will be other factors to consider when creating your designs.

Your mosaic may be intended for a predetermined place within a room, surrounded by other objects. It may also be used for a specific purpose, such as to contain water. Your designs should also take into account the fact that mosaic is long-lasting and the colours virtually permanent. Unlike textile, paper or even paint, stone, glass and ceramic do not disintegrate; nor do they break easily or fade. Once the setting medium is hard, changes cannot be made. These qualities are the great strengths of mosaic, but they also mean you cannot go over your work and cover it up.

All you need to do is be clear about what you want to achieve and how you want to realize it. Do this, and the materials, colour and style will marry happily with setting, mood and size to give you a mosaic of which you are proud. Before committing tesserae to adhesive, do consider the following design points.

Function

Always consider the main function of the mosaic: is it to be practical or decorative? Most mosaic is hardwearing and water-resistant, which makes it quite safe to use for items such as splashbacks behind the bathroom basin or kitchen sink, or for the floor of a hallway or conservatory. If the work is to withstand wear and tear from feet or soap and water, think about which materials will be best suited to your needs: glass, for example, is not so suitable for the passage of feet, bikes and perhaps the odd piece of garden equipment. However, if a purely decorative effect is what you are after, clearly these considerations do not apply and your choice is wider.

Location

Consider where the mosaic is to be positioned. Every aspect of the design – whether it is simple or complex, abstract or representational, the size, the colours to be used and the materials – is influenced by which room of the house the mosaic is intended for.

Focal point

Decide whether the mosaic is to stand out from or blend in with its surroundings. Will it be the focal point of a decorative scheme, or is it to go with established furniture or features? Your answers will determine how strong the design needs to be.

Mood

Consider the impact and mood the mosaic is to create. It is worth being clear at an early stage just how much of

a centrepiece you want your mosaic to be, as it is a strong medium that can easily upstage its surroundings. The mosaic can be as bold as you like, but its style should have a link with its situation. For example, a bright geometric mirror frame will jar in a guest bedroom that is decorated in soft florals; likewise a large panel in bright folk art reds and oranges might swamp a small but sophisticated all-white dining or living room.

Above: The earthy tones of this lamp stand complement the dusky yellow lampshade. Its spiral design is eye-catching, yet soothing, so it does not dominate the room.

Size

You need to decide on the size of the mosaic. Ensure that the design is in scale with the overall size: a tiny pattern will look out of place in a large mural, while a big pattern will look just as wrong in a tiny space.

Remember, too, that patterns or designs look larger the closer they are to your eye level. Look at one of the illustrations in this book at eye level, then put the same page on the floor; you will see how much detail is lost. Operate on a "less is more" principle and take out superfluous detail for smaller-scale pieces or those that will be viewed only from afar.

When designing a mosaic for an interior space, there are some important factors to think about.

Above: Satyr and Maenad – *a highly detailed replication by Salvatore Raeli of a 2nd-century mosaic panel from the House of the Faun, Pompeii, Italy.*

Left: Decorative mosaics can be used as accessories to coordinate with existing schemes and fittings. For example, this marine-inspired mirror frame echoes the coral marble sink unit.

To aid you in your planning and preparation and to help you avoid making time-consuming mistakes, there are some questions in the box opposite to consider. These will help you to be clear about the purpose of your design, taking into account whether it is a purely decorative or practical mosaic.

Mosaic is a bold medium, and you can cover large areas with it and create dramatic effects. In any home, it will be a strong feature. You want it to be striking but, if it is large, not to overpower its surroundings. Bear these factors in mind when beginning to plan work on design, colour, materials, size and location.

Light

Bear in mind the nature of daylight where you live: essentially blue in temperate areas and more red in tropical parts. Take some tesserae outside to see how natural light alters their colours. There is no reason why you cannot use strong, hot colours in temperate areas, but be aware of how vibrant they can look.

Siting

Clever positioning is part of a successful mosaic, where all aspects of its design (subject, pattern, framing, colour, texture and size) come together in the right setting. You might like to choose a design that is appropriate for the site, for example food in the kitchen, marine life in the bathroom, or vines in the dining room.

When you are working in a room on a ceiling or floor, consider the viewing lines. If the mosaic is to be seen at an angle, make sure it gives the best view. If the piece is in an architectural setting, make sure that the design is

points to consider when designing

- What is the mosaic's function?
- Which room is it going in?
- Is the room's colour scheme being built around the mosaic?
- If not, does the mosaic fit in with the existing scheme?
- Is the design you like appropriate to the room where you intend to place the mosaic?
- Are the weight of the object and the material used appropriate to its function and position?
- What happens if you decide to redecorate your home?
- Is the mosaic portable (wall-mounted, for instance, or on furniture)?
- If not, what will happen if you later want to move it to another place, or take it with you when you move into different accommodation?

Above: In a restrained modern setting this very striking mirror frame, designed by Marion Lynch, is all the ornamentation you need.

sympathetic to its surroundings. Mosaic-framed mirrors should be sited adjacent to windows, not opposite them, to achieve the best effects. Subtle colours should be positioned with care so the colours are enhanced, not lost by glare or bright light.

Scale

The size of your design is important, so this must be borne in mind when planning, and detail that will be lost at a distance must be eliminated. The importance of size applies equally to the actual size of the tesserae you are working with. Choose sizes that will

look right for their intended position: they must not be so large that they cannot cope with the design or pattern you want; neither should they be too small or they will tend to look untidy and ineffective.

White and dark grout

The effect of the mosaic varies dramatically depending on the colour of grout chosen: a white grout will make the overall effect very much lighter; a dark grout is deep and sombre but can create contrast. It is well worth testing out a small sample to decide which effect you want.

Materials and
Techniques

Mosaic is a versatile art form with great potential for personal creativity, and the range of materials available is visually exciting, colourful and tactile. And, as mosaic becomes more popular, the choice of material continues to grow. Planning projects and preparing the materials carefully enables you to create the mosaics you want, and this is followed by the vital grouting and cleaning stages, after which your mosaic is ready to be displayed.

The subtle sheen of marble, the opacity of smalti and the sheer opulence of gold leaf make these fascinating materials. These three mosaic tiles give a luxurious appearance to any mosaic.

Marble, Smalti and Gold Leaf

Each mosaic material has its own qualities that will influence the colour, style, look and texture of the finished piece. You can choose to work in just one medium or mix materials to create interesting texture and variety. Marble, smalti and gold leaf can work together to produce sumptuous results.

Marble

This is a natural material; it was used in Graeco-Roman times and is still associated with the luxurious qualities of modern Italian mosaics. Its hard and durable qualities make it excellent for use on floors. Marble is also a subtle material: it represents sheer beauty and natural elegance, and has a depth and timeless quality beyond any other material.

Above right: Marble comes in large slabs that can be cut into squares by hand to produce a more authentic style of mosaic.

Above far right: Smalti has been made for over 2,000 years. It is opaque and creates a wonderfully textural finish to mosaic.

Right: Machine-cut marble in regular squares on mesh or paper backing is effective for covering large areas.

Far right: A selection of tiles with gold and silver leaf twinkle with luxury and magic.

The colours are soft and the variations in tone are subtle: white, chalky pinks and rose, through to delicate greens, blues and blacks. Polishing intensifes the colours. When marble is cut, it has a crystalline appearance and the grains vary according to which part of the world the stone has come from.

For use in mosaics, marble is generally cut from rods with a hammer and hardie (a type of anvil). It is an expensive material, and this limits its use to the finest quality of mosaic.

You can also buy marble that has been machine-cut into regular squares. These squares are laid on to a paper backing, which can be soaked off. The handmade characteristic of the mosaic is lost in this form, but its quality is not impaired, and this is a cheaper form that can be used to cover large areas quickly.

Smalti

Traditionally made in Italy, smalti is opaque glass that is available in a great variety of colours. It is individually made, and the thickness, colour and size vary slightly each time. Each round slab, called a *pizze*, is made from molten glass fired with oxides, metals and powdered marble. Once it has cooled, it is cut into tesserae. It is often sold by the half kilo (1¼lb). *Smalti filati* are threads of glass rods of smalti used for micro-mosaics.

Designs made from smalti have a slightly uneven characteristic that creates a brilliant reflective surface. This bumpiness means that smalti mosaics are often not grouted and cannot be used on floors. Smalti comes in a superb range of colours, and any irregularities create character.

Gold leaf

This is the most opulent tile available to the mosaic artist. It is expensive, yet irresistible, and nothing can surpass its reflective quality. It can be used sparsely in a mosaic and still have a great impact and effect. The tesserae have a backing glass, which is usually

Above: Storing tiles in glass jars is a colourful and practical way to see what you have in stock.

turquoise, yellow or green. Then there is a layer of 24-carat gold leaf, which is protected with a thin layer of clear or coloured glass called the *cartellina*. The gold tesserae can have a smooth or bumpy surface.

Different variations are available with silver or copper leaf, a thin film of gold alloy or other metals. The colours of tile, ranging from deepest gold to vivid blues and greens, are formed when either the *cartellina* or the backing glass is altered.

With their luminous quality, wide range of colours and great choice of surface texture, glass tiles are invaluable to the mosaic artist. Ceramic tiles, which are widely available, offer additional textural variation.

Glass and Ceramic Tiles

These are usually made from vitreous glass and glazed and unglazed clay or porcelain, and come in small, regular tiles. They are laid on to mesh or brown paper to make up sheets measuring approximately 30 x 30cm (12 x 12in), which can be used to cover large areas without the tiles having to be laid individually. The range of materials is always expanding and there is a huge variety of colours and shapes to choose from.

Glass tiles

Vitreous glass is the most commonly used mosaic glass. Its production has been standardized, and it is therefore cheaper than smalti and more accessible to the amateur. It comes in sheets, and the individual tile is a regular square about 2 x 2cm (¾ x ¾in).

Right: Vitreous glass tiles come on sheets of mesh or brown paper, which are soaked off in warm water. The individual tiles can be clipped into smaller squares.

Above far right: Vitreous glass is a commonly used material; there is a lovely selection of colours. They are easy to clip with mosaic tile nippers.

Far right: Ceramic mosaic tiles come in many shapes and colours, and different kinds of textures.

The sheets can be used whole to cover large areas or split into sections for individual mosaics.

Glass is available in a wide variety of colours. The famous Bizzaria range has a grainy quality to the glass and offers a beautiful selection of tiles that have copper blended into the glass, creating a reflective quality that the other tiles can lack. Cutting the individual tiles into four creates the classic square tesserae; the glass is easy to clip and good for intricate designs.

There is a now also a new range of glass mosaic made in France. The colours are more rustic than Bizzaria. The glass is smooth and the concentration of the colour is even throughout, appearing like plastic. When these glass tiles are blended with the other glass ranges, they provide the mosaicist with a beautiful palette.

Glass is liable to chip or crack, so tile manufacturers have developed several types of sheet mosaic that are suitable for floors: these are non-slip and non-absorbent and meet many of the regulations associated with commercial properties.

Glass tiles can be shiny, round, square, bumpy, thick, thin, smooth or textured, and come in many different colours. Tiles for mosaic artists are like sweets for children: it is difficult to know which ones to choose. Stored in

clear glass jars, the colourful array can be quite spectacular.

Ceramic tiles

Mosaic ceramic tesserae are round or square and are made from porcelain. They are excellent for creating texture, as they can be glazed or unglazed: a combination of the two creates good surface interest.

Above: Display your mosaic tesserae in groups of colours in clear glass jars. You can easily see what you have available to use, and the gradations of tone and shade.

The colour is uniform in unglazed tiles, and the surface is likely to be matt and more porous than glazed tiles. Ceramic tiles are inexpensive and widely available from many craft stores.

All the materials mentioned so far build an image using mainly squares. Broken-up household tiles, smashed china and mirror, and pieces of stained glass, however, create mosaic pictures in a very different style.

Tiles, China, Mirror and Glass

Shiny household tiles, broken pieces of china, in all colours and shapes, pieces of reflective mirror and shimmering stained glass all bring a new creative freedom to mosaic-making.

Household tiles

Glazes on household tiles can be shiny, which enables you to play with the reflection of light in the design. When smashed up into irregular shapes, they are fantastic for working into abstract designs. The random shapes of the pieces also make them excellent for covering three-dimensional and sculptured surfaces. They are easy to handle and allow a freedom in expression that some regular square tiles lack, especially when working over curves.

Household tiles can reflect the contemporary aspect of mosaic. They offer enormous variety and versatility to the mosaic artist and it is possible to cover large areas cheaply with them.

China

The use of broken china is a wonderful way to recycle and make something beautiful out of otherwise useless items. A mosaic created with broken china is completely individual because no two pieces are likely to be the same.

China and crockery are not really suitable for intricate designs, but are wonderful for working with patterns

and texture. The curving nature of the material gives the final mosaic a textured finish. Odd pieces of pottery with quirky handles, lids and patterns can add some humour to a mosaic.

Mirror

You can buy mirror in sheets made up of small squares, or rectangles, or in large sheets that need to be smashed up. Mirror works very well scattered through a coloured mosaic. It also produces a fantastic effect when covering entire surfaces, especially sculptured forms. You can generally get offcuts from a glazier for free.

Stained glass

Walking into a stained glass supplier is like walking into an Aladdin's cave.

Above and above left: Plain household tiles are easy and cheap to obtain and can be easily cut to shape. They are good for sculptures and can be useful when you require the mosaic to be water-resistant.

Not only is there the most beautiful array of colours, but the glass has a wonderful shimmering quality to it, almost like jewels. There is even a stained glass that is iridescent and reflects light like mother-of-pearl.

Some types of stained glass are pieces of art in themselves. They can be used to cover whole surfaces for a luxurious finish or used in small areas to highlight details in a picture or an abstract pattern. Using stained glass in a mosaic design will create something extra special.

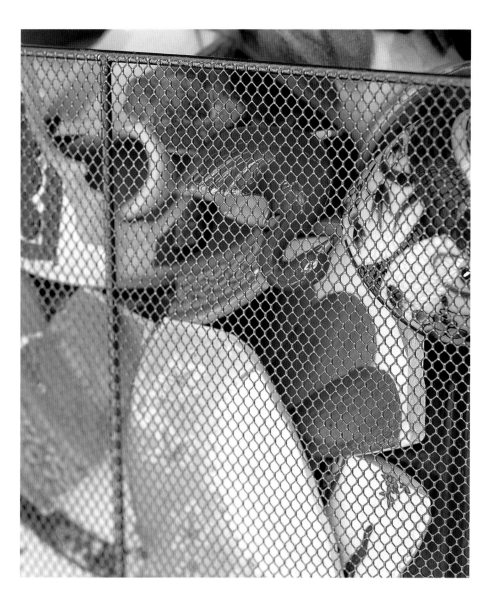

Right: The uneven quality of broken cups and plates creates texture, and the patterns and designs are also interesting to play around with in your own designs.

Below and below centre: Stained glass offers a beautiful array of colours and textures, and possesses wonderful reflective qualities. Each sheet of glass could be a piece of art in itself, and when it is broken up into small fragments provides a fantastic mosaic material.

Below far right: Recycling broken crockery to use in mosaic is an inventive and cheap source of materials. Collect pieces, and sort them by colour and pattern.

When making decorative mosaics, you can use both traditional materials and more unusual found and collected objects, ranging from shells and washed glass from beaches, to glass jewels and semi-precious stones.

Mixed Media

Using a variety of materials can bring personality and originality to mosaic designs. Mixed materials are particularly effective in sculptural mosaics and for creating a variety of textures and depth in two-dimensional work. It is also fun to gather a collection, such as natural materials from beaches or rivers, or old china from second-hand or thrift stores. There are no boundaries to what can be used, and it can be challenging to experiment with new methods and new materials.

Pebbles

Some of the earliest known mosaics were made from pebbles, and there is still a strong tradition in making pebble mosaics in Greece. In Lindos, Rhodes, you can find many pebble doorsteps and pavements.

Pebbles from the sea or rivers can be found in many subtle colour variations. They have a certain simplicity that is easy on the eye. They are long-lasting and it is possible to seal them, which makes them appear wet and the colours richer. Pebbles are traditionally used to cover large areas in gardens. They offer good drainage, and the simple designs look good without being overpowering.

Left: Glass beads with a flat metallic back used for making jewellery are brilliant for bringing a sparkle to mosaics.

Top: Stone, marble and slate can be cut into small pieces to create natural, subtle yet textural, mosaics.

Above: Shells come in beautiful soft colours and are traditionally used in grottoes or garden follies.

Top: Small pieces of washed glass can be added to mosaics for effect. Their soft colours give a gentle look.

Above: Washed glass and old pottery can often be found on a riverbank. Both will add character to a mosaic.

Top: Glass, plastic and antique beads all work well in mosaics, adding texture and colour to the work.

Above: Pebbles are good for creating simple, lasting designs and have natural muted tones and textural qualities.

Shells

Seashells, in their teeming variety of shapes and colours, have provided inspiration for craftspeople for centuries. The Chinese used mother-of-pearl for inlaying. Shells bedded into lime cement line the grottoes of Italian Renaissance gardens, and 18th-century European country house owners adorned their garden follies with them.

Salvaged materials

The edges of washed glass and pottery that have been smoothed and rounded by years of erosion in the water can be found on beaches and riverbanks. The effect of the water also softens the colours to create a gentle mosaic material. Collected or salvaged materials could include anything from old coins to forks and spoons. Metal foil, building blocks or even dice can be used.

Beads and jewels

Glass beads and jewels catch the light and twinkle. Their unevenness creates texture, which emphasizes the detail in a mosaic. Antique beads often have peculiarities within the glass that make them distinctive. You can buy jewels created for jewellery making that have a flat back, which makes them easier to lay, and placed in a mosaic they will add glints of colour.

Creating a design is fun, and collecting ideas in a scrapbook will be very useful for inspiring your projects. The design will affect your choice of materials, colours and style and the most suitable method of application.

Planning Projects

Take inspiration for your designs from books, magazines, other artists, nature or any other source that stimulates you. Keep any pictures or images that grab your attention for reference later. Stick them in a scrapbook and make notes about what you liked.

Drawings

The initial drawing will be only a guideline for your mosaic. Keep it simple and clear, with strong lines. If you cannot draw, trace an image or cut out a photocopy, and enlarge or adjust it to a suitable size and draw around it. It may be a good idea to make a few copies, so that you can try out different colour schemes before buying the tiles.

When you start applying the tesserae, your ideas may change as you work. This is all part of the evolutionary process of responding to the materials and their colour and texture.

It is not usually necessary to make all the design decisions at the beginning of the project. Creativity is a journey; allow the space during the process for new ideas and additions to unfold. When thinking about your design, bear in mind the colours, textures and contrast of the materials. Also, bear in mind how much time you want to spend on your mosaic, as this may influence the intricacy and complexity of the design.

Starting out

If the task is site specific, make an accurate template with graph paper or brown paper and/or take measurements before you start the detailed planning and work. Make clear notes while you are on site so it is easy to decipher the figures and information gathered when you are in your studio. It may help to photograph the site, too.

If you are a beginner, it is best to start with basic techniques and a small project, such as a pot stand, terracotta urn or small wall panel. As you become more confident, you can be more ambitious and explore your creativity.

Choosing tiles

The appearance of the mosaic is totally dependent on the materials you use. The design may even revolve around using a certain tile, the unique quality of which is your source of inspiration. Discovering how different materials work alone and with each other is an exciting aspect of mosaic artistry that takes time to master.

There is a fantastic range of tiles from all over the world in different colours, glazes and textures. You can use stone, with its soft colours, or choose from a lavish range of stained glass. There is no shortage of choice.

Aside from aesthetic decisions, there are various factors to take into account when choosing. The cost could be a consideration; for example marble is a very beautiful and durable material, but it is very expensive, while porcelain is a much cheaper alternative.

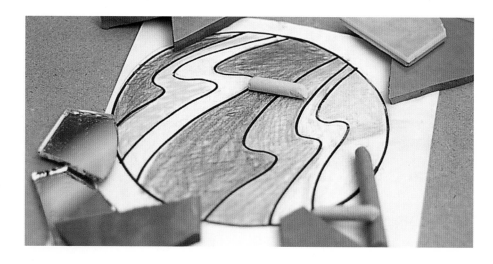

Left: It is useful to make a simple line drawing first using a soft pencil, then emphasize the lines with a black pen and shade in the colours to be mosaiced.

Above: There is a huge range of mosaic tiles to choose from. Vitreous glass tiles, shown here, are best suited to indoor work.

Left: Tile sample boards are a useful way of choosing colours and tiles for a project. Tile suppliers have a wealth of knowledge, and it is important to check with them that the tiles you choose suit the project you are undertaking.

Qualities of tiles

Not all tiles are suitable for all situations, so it is vital to make the right choice if your mosaic is to last. Each tile and material varies, so check their qualities and uses when you buy them.

Glass tiles or stained glass would be damaged quickly if positioned on a floor and exposed to high heels. Glazes also come in varying levels of hardness; a soft glaze would restrict the tile use to inside. A harder glaze can be used on the floor, and a frost-proof tile can be used outside. The fired clay that lies under the glaze also has its own individual qualities, such as absorbency, which can affect whether the tiles are suitable for a shower or bathroom.

choosing the right technique

Each project is different and no task is approached in exactly the same way. You need to decide which technique to use and the suitable fixing agents that are required. Here are some questions that you should consider before starting:

- Where is the piece to be finally positioned?
- Will you work directly, for example on to the pot?
- Will you choose a semi-indirect method, for example on to mesh, which is good for a floor panel?

- Is the site accessible, or is it easier to make the mosaic off-site?
- How durable does the mosaic need to be?
- Does the mosaic need to be water-resistant, waterproof, weather- or frost-proof?

While a small project could be made in a kitchen or a shed, it is advisable to allocate a special space in which to work, giving you a clean area for drawing and a workbench or table for assembling the mosaic.

Creating a Workspace

The workspace is your own creative environment, so some wall space should be allocated for displaying your finished mosaics and any images that inspire you. Shelving will be needed, to store books, files, tools and materials, and a water supply is essential.

Posture

The most comfortable way to mosaic is definitely working at an easel or a table. It is important to have the seat or stool at a suitable height. It is worth spending time getting this right so that a good posture can be maintained and you can avoid shoulder and back strain.

Lighting

Ideally, the table or workbench should be placed near a natural source of light. Daylight is the best way to see true colour. When light is limited or when you are working at night, daylight bulbs are ideal. It is best to have more than one light source to avoid shadows.

Storage

When organizing materials, it is a good idea to build shelving and store tiles in glass or clear plastic jars, so it is easy to see how much stock you have and all the different colours. Tools are expensive and rust easily, so keep them clean and dry. Adhesives and grouts solidify if they get wet, so they must all

be stored in a damp-free area, preferably in sealed containers. Most chemicals have a limited shelf life and can go off, so should be checked regularly.

Large mosaics

When working on a mosaic that is too big for a table or easel, you should work on, or at least prepare the design on, the floor. You will need a hard

Left: Larger projects can be planned on the floor or in an area where it is possible to see the whole design.

safety

These are sensible precautions you can take to avoid injuring yourself:

- Wear goggles when cutting materials to avoid getting fragments in your eyes. Hold the mosaic tile nippers away from your face.
- Wear a face mask when cutting wood or mixing powder to avoid inhaling fine powder into sinuses and lungs.
- Wear hardwearing gloves when cutting wire and use rubber or latex gloves when mixing up powders, and also when grouting, cleaning or sculpting. Your hands

will get dry and sore if they come into contact with water and adhesives for too long. It is also recommended to wear thin latex gloves when making mosaics. Take care, and keep antiseptic cream, plasters and hand cream on your shelving.

- Hold mosaic tile nippers at the far end of the handle to avoid hand blisters.
- Always clean and vacuum the work area regularly to avoid an unnecessary build-up of dust.
- Create your mosaic with care for the safety of those around you, as well as yourself.

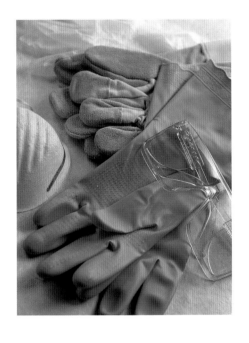

surface, so if the floor is carpeted, use a large piece of wood. If you are using mesh or brown paper, you should draw up the design and get a clear understanding of the whole image. Then you can cut the image into fragments and work in sections on the workbench.

If you need to see the whole design develop, it is best to work on the floor and protect the surrounding surfaces with plastic sheeting. This can be hard on the back, so you should take regular breaks and have a good stretch.

Preparing for work

Once you have chosen where and how to work and what to mosaic, you should gather all the required tools and materials together, mix enough fixing agents for the immediate work and prepare a good range of tiles before commencing.

Keep the work area clean, sweeping away loose fragments regularly. It also makes good sense to keep coloured tiles in some kind of order, placing different tiles, colours and shapes in separate small piles, for ease of use. When working with cement-based adhesive, clean off any excess while it is damp; if left overnight, the cement will harden and become very difficult to remove from the surface it is on.

Cleaning up

Sweep up or vacuum at the end of each session, as fragments get everywhere and can be sharp. Cleaning and reorganizing will also make the next day's work much easier. If different

Above: Good light, a work surface and seating at the right height for good posture are essential for comfortable and productive mosaic-making.

Above left: Gloves, goggles and face masks should be worn to protect against any injury or harmful inhalation caused by sharp chips or ground glass or tile.

cement-based adhesives and grouts are allowed to mix in the drains, this can cause serious blockages and endless problems. When cleaning mixing bowls that held these materials, therefore, always scrape out and throw away as much excess as possible, before washing away the residue. Placing gauze over the plug can avoid the need to clean the drains regularly.

The materials for a mosaic usually need some form of preparation for the work. Tiles can be smashed, nipped or sawn, glass cut and marble or smalti reduced to the correct size pieces with a hammer and hardie.

Preparing Materials

By preparing and clipping the materials you will be using before you start the mosaic – in the same way as a painter would mix a palette of paints – you will be free to concentrate on laying the mosaic design.

Sheet mosaic

Many mosaic tiles come on sheets, either on fibreglass mesh or on brown paper; the tiles are about 2cm (¾in) square and the sheets are approximately 30cm (12in) square. These are useful for laying a large area.

When making smaller mosaics using sheet mosaic, you should take the tiles off their backing. To remove the tiles from sheets formed with brown paper or mesh, soak the whole sheets in clean warm water. When the glue has dissolved, the tiles will slip off the backing material easily.

Smashed ceramic tiles

Antonio Gaudí is famous for his extensive use of mosaic in his fairytale buildings in Barcelona. They are very colourful and predominantly use ceramic tiles smashed into small fragments. Ceramic tiles come in an enormous range of colours, tones, textures and glazes, and are suitable for both interior and exterior use, as many are frost-proof. They are fun and easy to work with.

Clipping tiles

Mosaic tile nippers are the essential tool for any mosaicist, and are good for clipping most materials. With practice, intricate shapes can be achieved.

The mosaic nippers should be held at the end of the handles for the best possible leverage. The rounded side of the head is placed over the tile, which need be inserted only a few millimetres. To cut the tile in half, the nippers are positioned in the centre of the tile with the head pointing in the direction the cut is needed. Holding the opposite edge of the tile between thumb, fore-finger and index finger will stabilize it. The ends of the handles are then presssed together.

Goggles are essential, as initially the tiles seem to fly all over the place. With practice, however, it becomes possible to control the cuts, and the fingers support the bits in place. If the cut goes astray, the excess can be nibbled away on the edge of the tile.

Cutting and sawing tiles

A hand tile cutter is the tool traditionally used for cutting tiles, and it is available from do-it-yourself stores. It

smashing ceramic tiles

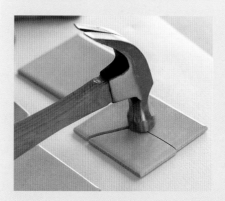

1 Wearing goggles and protective gloves, smash the tiles with a small hammer, aiming at the centre of the tile. To make these fragments smaller, gently smash with a hammer in the centre of each fragment.

2 Pieces can fly all over the place if you hit the tile too hard, so for protection, cover the tiles with a cloth and wear goggles. Use the mosaic nippers to shape the ceramics into the size and style required.

Right: Glass and mirror can be cut with a glass cutter. The surface is scored lightly, using a metal rule as a guide, then broken.

Far right: A hammer and hardie are used to break thick materials, such as stone and smalti, into pieces.

will cut straight lines on tiles, though its use is limited to ceramic tiles with a soft clay base.

Hard floor tiles or stone need to be cut with a wet tile saw. This specialized piece of equipment is essential for certain tasks, such as cutting thin strips of marble, which are then made into the correct size for mosaicing with a hammer and hardie. It is possible to hire wet tile saws.

The saw cuts the material with a metal disc that is revolved by a motor and kept cool with water. As the tile hits the blade, the water can spray out, making this quite a messy but effective technique needing protective clothing.

Cutting glass

A glass cutter is used for cutting straight lines or large shapes in stained glass and mirror.

Right: (from the top) Tile cutters, for cutting straight lines; a tile scorer; mosaic tile nippers, for cutting tiles into shapes; a craft (utility) knife; and a glass cutter for cutting glass and mirror.

The surface should be scored lightly with the cutter, then the ball of the cutter used to tap the underside gently; it will crack along the line. Tile nippers are good for making smaller cuts and detailed shapes.

Goggles and gloves should be worn when handling glass and mirror, since even the smallest splinters cut easily.

Cutting stone and smalti

A hammer and hardie are the traditional tools for cutting stone and smalti, both of which are too thick for modern tile clippers. The material is held over the chisel between the thumb and forefinger and the hammer swung down on to this point. With practice, accurate cutting is obtained.

Mosaics can be laid on to a variety of different surfaces, and, as long as the correct procedures are followed, they will be hardwearing and waterproof and have a professional-quality finish.

Preparation and Fixing

Traditional mosaics were laid on to a cement bed. Now, we can also mosaic on to all sorts of different surfaces, such as wood, old furniture, plaster, ceramic, terracotta or fibreglass.

Bases

Unless working with a sculptured form, you should work on to a flat, even surface for a professional-quality mosaic. Uneven surfaces should be sanded down. If working on to cement, a new surface should be laid; self-levelling cement is an easy option.

The base or surface should be rigid. For example, floorboards are flexible, and any mosaic laid on them will lift if there is movement. So a thin layer of wood should be cut to fit and screwed in evenly to cover the entire surface.

Wood is a very good base, but if the mosaic will come into contact with water, the wood must be exterior grade, such as marine ply.

Priming surfaces

Most working surfaces, such as wood, concrete, terracotta urns, old furniture or plaster, are porous, so the surface must be sealed with diluted PVA (white) glue (see box below). This greatly improves the sticking power of adhesive and makes the final mosaic more hardwearing and waterproof.

Before sealing, it is important to ensure that the surface is clean of all loose debris and hair. Smooth surfaces, such as wood or fine plaster, should be scored with a sharp implement, such as a bradawl or craft (utility) knife. On more slippery surfaces, such as plastics or existing tiles, a special two-part resin primer can be brushed on to provide a key. It creates a surface to which an adhesive can easily attach.

Diluted PVA glue can also be used to coat terracotta pots in order to make them frost-resistant.

Fixing methods

Once the surface has been properly prepared, there are various ways to fix the tiles. Choosing which technique to use depends partly on where the mosaic is situated and partly on personal preference. The direct method involves placing the material straight on to the working surface. The indirect method involves creating the mosaic off-site, then installing it. Two semi-indirect methods are worked on to paper or mesh off-site and then fitted into the cement on-site, so combining aspects of both methods.

Traditional stone and smalti mosaics were laid straight on to a bed of cement. Modern materials, however, are often much thinner, and need to be stuck as well as embedded.

priming wood

1 Take a craft (utility) knife and score the surface of the wood, creating a key. This improves the grip between the wood and the adhesive.

2 Mix up PVA (white) glue with water in a ratio of 1 part glue to 3 parts water. Apply this evenly with a dense sponge or a paintbrush.

Right: You will need some, if not all, of these tools to prepare surfaces and apply adhesive. Clockwise from top left: hard bristle brush, paintbrush for glue, notched trowel, hammer, chisel, flexible knife, dustpan and brush, rubber spreader and adhesive applicator.

Direct method

This method involves simply sticking the tesserae, face up, on to the base, which has been covered with a layer of cement-based tile adhesive. It is good for working on to wood or sculptured forms, when working with smashed ceramic tiles, washed glass, tiles of different heights, or when covering large areas. It is also good to work directly into adhesive because it avoids having to spend extra time fitting and allows the design to develop in the environment where the mosaic is situated.

The direct method is easiest to start with and recommended for beginners.

Indirect method

Originally, this technique was devised as a way of making large-scale mosaics off-site, so that they could be moved ready-made, then laid in position. The design would be sectioned into manageable areas, and each area made into a slab. It is equally useful, however, for mosaics that cannot be laid directly due to an awkward location.

working with cement-based tile adhesive

1 Mix white cement-based tile adhesive with water in the ratio of 2½ parts powder to 1 part water, until you have a smooth consistency. Choose and prepare the tiles you are going to use. Apply adhesive to the base with a flexible knife.

2 Stick the tesserae into the adhesive, ensuring good contact by pushing them in with your fingertips. If you use too much adhesive, the excess will squeeze through the gaps and get messy, but if you use too little, the tesserae will fall off.

A wooden frame is made to the size of the finished slab, and greased internally with petroleum jelly. The mosaic is appplied to a piece of brown paper marked with the dimensions of the slab, using the semi-indirect brown paper method (see right).

When the tesserae are dry, the frame is placed over the paper and dry sand sprinkled over the design and nudged into the crevices with a soft brush. The frame is then filled with mortar. The surface is smoothed, then covered with damp newspaper and polythene (polyethylene) sheeting and left to dry slowly for five to six days.

When the mortar is dry, the slab and frame are turned over and the brown paper dampened with a wet sponge, then peeled away. The frame is unscrewed and the slab removed.

Brown paper method

This reverse technique involves gluing the tesserae into position off-site, then setting them into adhesive on-site, cutting up the sheets of mosaic if needed.

When using this technique, the tesserae are glued face down on brown paper with PVA (white) glue; if they are uneven in any way, the irregularity will occur on the underside of the mosaic, making this method ideal for mosaics requiring a smooth surface.

The front of the mosaic is invisible during the design process, so this method is limited to tesserae that are coloured right through.

Once the mosaic sheet is pressed into the waiting adhesive, and been left to dry for 24 hours, the brown paper is soaked off with a wet sponge.

Mesh method

In this second semi-indirect method, fine-weave fibreglass mesh acts as a perfect base for the mosaic. The tesserae are stuck face up on to the mesh, so it

the direct method using PVA glue

   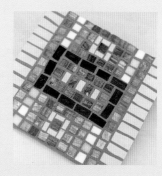

1 Cut a piece of wood to the desired size. Clip a selection of tiles into quarters and halves. Experiment with the tesserae; the design does not need to be complicated.

2 Once you are happy with the design, use a small brush to apply the PVA (white) glue to the back of the tesserae, and stick them in place and leave to dry.

3 Mix up some grey powder grout with water in the ratio of 3½ parts grout to 1 part water. Apply with your fingertips, wearing rubber (latex) gloves.

4 Wipe down the surface with a damp sponge to remove all traces of grout on the tesserae. Once the grout is dry, polish the tiles with a dry, soft cloth.

is possible to see the mosaic design developing and taking shape. If the mosaic is large, it can be cut up and transported easily. When the tesserae are secure on the mesh, it is pressed, face up, into the adhesive and left to dry.

Cement-based tile adhesives

There is a vast range of modern cement-based tile adhesives for use on both direct and indirect mosaics. They come in a variety of shades, mainly white and grey. Your choice of colour will be influenced by what colour you want to grout in: grey for grey, black or dark colours; white for lighter shades.

Medium-strength adhesive comes in tubs ready-mixed, which is fine for decorative pieces or if the mosaic does not need to be particularly waterproof.

Most large tile companies have their recommended range of cement-based adhesive and additives. It is worth asking which materials are most suitable for the job you are undertaking. There is a variety of products for all situations, from exterior frost-proof, cement-based adhesives through to flexible liquid additives, such as admix, which can be added for extra protection against movement or to make the adhesive suitable for a shower.

PVA glue

This is good for sticking tiles directly on to wood, when it should be used undiluted. For priming or sealing, dilute PVA (white) glue 3:1 with water. It is water-based, so its use is limited to internal use only. It dries slowly, so tiles may be repositioned.

Epoxy resin glue

This is a strong glue made up of two separate components: the hardener and the resin. It is good for use in underwater locations or in damp places, but it has a limited working time and is sticky and toxic, so a face mask should be worn. Epoxy resin glue is useful when working with the direct method as it sets in just four hours, reducing drying times drastically.

Right: This soft mesh is used for subtle relief work, while chicken wire is more effective for larger-scale sculpting. Big exterior sculpting can be formed with bricks or breezeblocks (cinderblocks) then covered with a layer of tile adhesive.

Far right: In the mesh method, the mosaic pieces are glued, face up, straight on to the fibreglass mesh.

Grouting is incredibly satisfying: it unifies the mosaic and blends the images and colours. Designs that felt garish or too busy are softened, and patterns that work with movement come to life.

Grouting

On a practical level, grouting is when the gaps between the tiles are filled with a cement mortar that has a different quality to the adhesives. The process strengthens the mosaic and makes it waterproof. Grouting ensures that mosaic can be a functional art form that can be used in swimming pools, showers, water features, external wall murals or lavish floors.

Grout comes either ready-mixed or in a powder and in a variety of colours. There are also powdered stains that you can add to create almost any colour you want. The colour you choose will have a profound effect on the colours and look of the finished mosaic. Some of these differences can be seen in the four panels below. The grid of dark grey grout overpowers the neutral grey tiles, and the white grout is also very strong. The light grey grout works well with the tiles, as there is balance, while the beige grout warms the neutral tiles.

Note that white grout will blend with pale tiles, lighten darker colours and contrast blacks, while black grout will deepen blacks and blues, make reds and greens really rich and contrast with white. The qualities and varieties are endless, giving you great scope for creativity.

Grouting is a messy job, especially if stains are used, so clothes and surroundings should be well protected and rubber (latex) gloves should be worn to protect the hands.

When to grout

The finished mosaic should be grouted when the tile adhesive is dry. Before

Right: These four panels of neutral vitreous glass mosaic were grouted in four different shades: clockwise from top left, beige, dark grey, light grey and white.

Below: Grout comes in different colours, which can dramatically alter the finished look of the mosaic.

being grouted, small mosaics can be gently shaken to remove loose adhesive, and any loose tiles can be re-adhered. On larger-scale mosaics, light vacuuming can be effective.

On a large-scale project, the whole surface should not be grouted in one go, because when you start to clean off the grout, the first areas may have already dried. One section should be grouted at a time, then cleaned off before the next section is begun. The grout should be left to dry for 24 hours until it is completely hard.

Above: For grouting and cleaning your mosaics, you will need a mixing trowel, a grout spreader, some cleaning cloths, a sponge, a bowl and protective sheeting.

Above: Wear rubber (latex) gloves and grout your mosaic using a rubber spreader. Rub the grout into any gaps using your fingertips.

grouting and cleaning

1 When the mosaic is being laid, adhesive can squeeze through the gaps between the tesserae. Scrape this away with a blade or craft (utility) knife. Then ensure that the mosaic is clean.

2 Wearing rubber (latex) gloves, mix together the powdered grout and clean water in a bowl. Follow the manufacturer's instructions to achieve the right consistency.

3 Apply the grout over the mosaic, using your fingers, a grout spreader or a rubber spreader. Push the paste into the gaps and smooth it evenly over the whole surface.

4 Wipe away any excess grout with a damp sponge. After 10 minutes, any remaining excess grout can be rubbed away easily with a dry cloth. (If left much longer, remove with a nailbrush or paint scraper.)

Once the colours and the design of the mosaic have been revealed by the cleaning process, attention must be paid to where and how to present the finished work, how to light it and how to maintain its beauty.

Finishing Your Work

If the tesserae of the mosaic have a shiny glaze, the grout will have come off easily with the sponging process. Matt porcelain, however, holds the grout, making it harder to clean.

It is possible to buy an acid called patio cleaner, used by builders for cleaning cement off brickwork. When diluted with warm water, it is very effective for removing resilient grout. If sponged or poured on to the mosaic, it will make a fizzing noise as it eats away at the grout left on the surface of the tiles. After a few minutes, the dirty water can be sponged away. Resistant areas can be removed with a paint-scraper or abrasive paper (sandpaper), before being polished with clean cloths.

Sealing

Stone and pebbles look richer when sealed, appearing slightly wet and retaining their subtlety of tone without the addition of a varnish or shine to the surface. Sealants come in matt or shiny varieties.

Beeswax can be rubbed on to matt tiles to give them a deeper colour. Terracotta tiles need to be treated with linseed oil. This is flammable, so always dispose of cloths that the oil comes into contact with carefully.

Siting

There are no hard-and-fast rules about where to site your mosaic; it is a matter of judgement and common sense, which you must learn to trust. Asking someone to hold the mosaic in place so you can have a look is always wise. You can usually tell when the site is right. If you are unsure, you can swap with your helper to ask their opinion.

Aside from the positioning of the mosaic, the colour of the surrounding walls must be taken into consideration. You do not want the walls to clash with the mosaic, or for them to overpower it.

Hanging

A small mosaic can be hung like a picture, using wire and picture hooks. Hanging a larger, heavier mosaic, however, requires more thought.

Far left: This colourful panel is lightened by the white grout, and the glazed tiles laid in a Gaudí-style mosaic have a fresh flowing feel. To clean, first spray the mosaic with glass cleaner. Any proprietary window cleaner will do. If you do not have this, use some water with vinegar added to reduce smearing.

Left: Polish with a clean dry cloth, preferably a lint-free one, and you should achieve a good shine on the glass and the glazed ceramic tiles. The colours weave into each other, while the mirror and glass balls make shimmering focal points within the mosaic.

It is important to find out whether the wall you intend to fix the mosaic to can hold the weight. Plasterboard (gypsum board) will not, so if it is a partition wall, the mosaic must be fixed to a supporting strut.

When fixing into brick or plaster, you will need to drill holes, using a drill bit that is compatible with the size of screw you have chosen. The correct position for the fixings should be marked on the wall with a pen. Wall plugs (plastic anchors) should be placed in the drilled holes to give the screws something to grip on to, then the mosaic can be hung in place.

Mosaic panels can also be fixed to the wall with mirror plates. Protruding mirror plates are fitted to the wood at the edge of the panel and then the mirror plates are screwed to the wall. Those with a keyhole opening are fitted to the back; they then slot over screws inserted into the wall.

Lighting

Mosaics nearly always look their best in natural light, with its soft tones. Yet the night-time light is important and needs consideration.

A mosaic could be lit with a spotlight fixed on the ceiling or a traditional picture light. It is important not to over-light and bleach out the colours and subtle reflective quality of the tiles. Different colours and wattages of bulb, as well as different angles and distances, should all be tried.

Maintenance

The best way to maintain a mosaic is to clean it regularly, so avoiding the build-up of resilient dirt. A floor mosaic should be swept and mopped with a gentle cleaning agent, making sure the dirty water is removed properly. Decorative mosaics should be dusted and cleaned using glass cleaner and a dry cloth. Bathroom mosaics should be cleaned as any other tile.

Above: These are some of the tools you may need when siting and installing your mosaic. Clockwise, from top right: saw, hammer, abrasive paper (sandpaper), wire (steel) wool, U-shaped hooks, pliers, screwdriver, picture wire, picture hooks, hanging hooks, screw eyes, screws, wall plugs (plastic anchors) and eraser.

If the mosaic has got really dirty, the patio cleaner referred to opposite should be used, though it may be necessary to re-grout after cleaning. If the correct maintenance steps are taken, the mosaic could last for a millennium.

Ornaments

Ornaments are not just the frippery that they are made out to be. Often they are useful objects that we need to have around the house, but that can be disguised or decorated in such a way as to make them a pleasure to have around. Even those objects which are solely decorative do perform a psychological function in brightening up our everyday lives. All the projects have been graded from one to five, one being the easiest.

Creating beautiful decorative accessories for the home offers a limitless supply of design opportunities for the mosaicist: from simple objects, such as a small frame, to more advanced pieces, such as a lamp base.

Decorative Accessories

Mosaic is an effective disguise for many everyday objects, transforming the mundane or mass-produced into something original. Containers, in particular, make excellent subjects for mosaic decoration. Plant pots, terracotta urns, candle-holders, vases and bowls are just a few suggestions.

Smaller ornaments

Excellent hunting grounds for objects to mosaic – such as picture frames, plain wooden boxes, old pots and bowls – are car-boot sales, junk (curio) shops and even house clearance auctions. "Job lot" boxes of assorted odds and ends can be picked up extremely cheaply. These do not require a huge commitment in terms of time, effort or cost of materials, making them good items on which to practise your ideas and techniques. The objects can be functional or purely decorative.

A small picture frame, decorative box or mirror tile would be ideal choices to start with, since they are regular in shape, can be laid flat and are easy to work with. A set of mats or coasters would be an easy way of experimenting with colour and patterns before embarking on larger projects. Some candle holders in a wide range of patterns and colours, a group

Below left: Gentle spiralling bands of mosaic cover this tall terracotta urn.

Below centre: Pots of fresh herbs in the kitchen become decorative objects in their own right.

Below right: Squares of textured coloured glass cast beautiful patterns when a candle is lit in this mosaic candle-holder.

Above: This large, striped, stained-glass mosaic bowl was made by Martin Cohen.

of cheerful bowls or pots and simple mirror frame would expand your repertoire a little, while still being fairly simple projects that are easy to work.

A contemporary mosaic bowl can be made by buying a shallow, light, wooden, metal or plastic shape to which you can adhere mosaic on the inside only. This will give you a stable base on to which to add your pattern.

Larger ornaments

Once you have gained confidence, you may feel ready to try some items that are more ambitious in terms of scale or complexity.

A tray for the kitchen gives scope for quite a large design, with a ready-made border formed by the sides. A floral lamp base for the sitting room worked on a breezeblock (cinderblock) combines both artistry and some basic wiring, while a spiral lamp stand makes use of an old carpet tube.

The cosmic clock – at home in any room – could be an inspiration for many different clock designs. A hole must always to drilled to allow for the spindle to be pushed through to the front, and the mosaic design must avoid tiling over this hole. The surface decoration needs to be designed to allow for the function of the clock and the movement of the hands.

Looking to the bedroom, the floral trinket box transforms a plain wooden box into a work of great beauty.

The reflective and shimmering qualities of vitreous glass mosaic tiles work well with mirrored glass and will beautifully adorn any interior. Mirror frames can be made in many different shapes and sizes.

Mirror Frames

Mirror frames can be bought ready made, or they can be made from many diverse materials that can be customized with mosaic. They can be flat or include three-dimensional or sculptural elements. They can also be as extravagant or simple as you want. They provide an excellent platform for self-expression, and you can explore combinations of colour and texture to create collage-like effects.

Right: This large, curved mirror was inspired by a Gustav Klimt painting, reflected in the shape of the design. Its use of flowing lines of gold smalti, broken up in a rhythmic pattern, makes a very decorative and individual piece, designed by Norma Vondee.

Below: A pair of complementary circular mirrors are given extra interest by having the mirrors placed off-centre.

Left: Two differently toned variations of the same style mirror echoing the soft, warm tones of the wooden floor.

Opposite: This large, curvaceous mirror by Celia Gregory was made from washed glass collected from the banks of the River Thames, and contrasts with the angular shape of the fireplace. The soft greens beautifully complement the whites and neutral tones of the room.

Squares of coloured glass cast beautiful patterns at night, when the candle is lit in a darkened room. Practise the glass-cutting technique first on scraps of clear glass.

Stained-glass Candle-holder

You will need
Pencil
Ruler
Graph paper
Sheets of textured coloured glass
Glass cutter
Pliers
Clear all-purpose adhesive
Clear glass candle-holder
Tile grout
Flexible knife
Sponge or soft cloth

1 Using a pencil and ruler, draw a grid of 4cm (1½in) squares on graph paper.

2 Place each sheet of coloured glass over the grid. Following your drawn lines, score vertical lines with a glass cutter (see Materials and Techniques).

3 Using pliers, and holding the glass carefully, snap the glass along the scored lines into neat, evenly sized pieces.

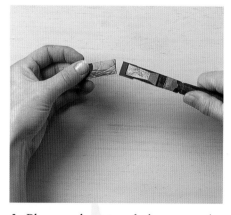

4 Place each strip of glass over the paper grid, score horizontal lines and snap off the squares with the pliers, until you have enough squares to cover the candle-holder.

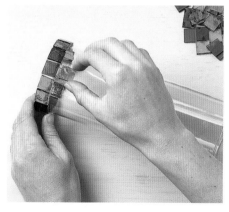

5 Stick the squares of glass in neat rows around the candle-holder with clear adhesive, alternating the colours, and leaving a tiny gap between each tile. Using a flexible knife, spread the tile grout over the mosaic, filling all the gaps. Rub the excess grout off with a damp sponge or soft cloth. Leave to dry completely before using.

This unusual design is shown here as a mirror frame, but a similar frame could just as easily be used to frame a photograph or favourite picture. Only two colours are used, although the grouting is a third element.

Squiggle Frame

You will need

9mm (³⁄₈in) thick plywood

Jigsaw (saber saw)

PVA (white) glue

Paintbrush

Glazed ceramic household tiles:

6 blue, 10 black

Dish towel

Hammer

Pencils

Tracing paper

Tape measure

Carbon paper

Thick felt-tipped pen

Tile adhesive

Admix

Tile grout

Rubber spreader

Sponge

Soft cloth

Mirror

1 Cut a sheet of plywood measuring 50 x 70cm (20 x 28in) with a jigsaw (saber saw). Using a large brush, prime the wood by coating it all over with diluted PVA (white) glue. Leave it to dry for 24 hours.

2 Place two blue tiles face down on a dish towel and fold over the edges. Using a hammer, smash the tiles repeatedly, checking from time to time until they are roughly broken into manageable fragments, keeping the blue and black pieces in separate piles.

3 Draw around the plywood sheet on a large sheet of tracing paper, then draw an inner rectangle of 39 x 60cm (16 x 24in). Sketch one scroll design on the tracing paper, then use sheets of carbon paper to transfer your design on to the plywood, flipping the tracing paper to repeat a mirror image another five times. Go over with a thick pen.

4 Mix some tile adhesive with admix, then spread it 3mm (⅛in) thick over a small section of one of the scrolls, removing any excess. Working from the scroll edge out, fill in the blue tiles, and repeat until the frame is covered. Allow 24 hours for the adhesive to dry.

5 Spread some tile grout over the mosaic with a rubber spreader, using a circular motion. Continue until the grout fills all the gaps and is level with the tesserae. Sponge away any surface grout with a damp sponge. Allow to dry for 1 hour, then polish with a dry, soft cloth to rub off any residual grout. Glue the mirror in place.

Small mosaic tiles make an attractive Mediterranean-style frame. To keep the project simple, plan the dimensions of the frame to suit the size of the tiles, so avoiding having to cut and fit odd-shaped pieces.

Mediterranean Mirror

You will need

2cm (¾in) thick MDF (medium-density fiberboard)

Pencil

Saw

Drill

Jigsaw (saber saw)

Wood glue

White acrylic primer

Paintbrush

Tile adhesive

Grout spreader

Vitreous glass mosaic tiles: blues, greens, and yellows

Tile grout

Soft cloth

Mirror

Narrow frame moulding

2 ring screws and brass picture wire

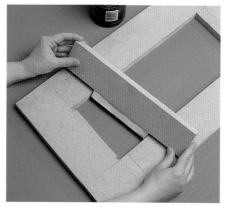

1 Draw a rectangular frame on MDF (medium-density fiberboard). Cut it out using a saw. Drill corner holes for the centre and cut this out with a jigsaw (saber saw). Cut out a shelf and glue it to the frame with wood glue. Allow to dry.

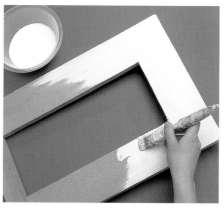

2 Prime both sides of the frame and shelf with white acrylic primer to seal it. Allow to dry. Apply tile adhesive to a small area of the frame, using the fine-notched side of a grout spreader.

3 Apply a random selection of tiles, leaving a 2mm (¹⁄₁₆in) gap between them. Complete the frame, working on a small area at a time. Tile the edges with a single row of tiles.

4 Allow the tile adhesive to dry. Wearing rubber (latex) gloves, spread grout over the surface of the tiles with the grout spreader. Scrape off the excess with the spreader and clean off any remaining grout with a soft cloth. Leave to dry thoroughly.

5 Place the mirror face down on the back of the frame and secure it with narrow frame moulding, glued in place with wood glue. Allow to dry.

Screw two ring screws in place on the back of the mirror, more than halfway up the side towards the top, and tie on picture wire securely, to hang it on a wall.

Tile Mastic

Mastic is a very sticky adhesive. It comes premixed and is readily available at most home improvement stores. It usually comes in a small bucket of varying sizes with a snap top lid. It has a very long shelf life when kept closed.

- **Read the manufactures instructions!** (you'll hear me say this a lot.) Each brand has it's own recommendations. Look for Type I or better for maximum water resistance.
- Even when using Type I, mastic is for **INDOOR** applications only and where it will not be exposed to moisture.
- Typically white or light in color, the color can be altered using liquid pigments. This is especially helpful when you are using on a project that you don't plan on grout, such as Italian Smalti.
- Works great on vertical surfaces where sliding can be an issue.
- It's thick texture allows you to build-up for use with materials of different thicknesses.
- May be use to adhere to wood, drywall, Formica, ceramic.
- Mastic is **NOT** intended for use on floors. It will become brittle and break down under pressure.
- For art projects use a palette knife to spread in small areas.

Other Sticky Stuff

This section covers the rest of the sticky stuff, such as silicones, epoxies and construction adhesives. Although these adhesives do not have a regular place in our world of mosaics there are often applications when you need "something" else.

Silicones - This category includes adhesives like **Lexel**, Clear liquid Nails, etc. They are typically clear, very flexible and readily available at home improvement centers. They contain serious chemicals and may have strong fumes. Lexel is my silicone of choice, as it seems to be less "fumey". I have actually gotten what I call a "silicone hangover" from using other brands. Read the manufactures directions for uses and precautions.

1.	Silicones work great on flexible backing such as metal. Most are "all weather" and can be used on exterior projects. Allows for expansion and contraction in different temperatures. I have successfully used **Lexel** on several metal and glass bases that "live" outside in Wisconsin.

2.	Clear silicones work well when adhering glass to glass or any slick surface. May be used to on hurricane lamps and votives, etc.

Epoxy - This is a very strong quick setting two part adhesive reserved for unique applications which include things like gluing cup handles, heavy pieces that just slide, etc. To be used when you need a quick set.

1.	Epoxy is a two part glue (resin + hardener) that must be mixed. My favorite is Power Poxy. It is very thick and sets quickly.

2.	Epoxy has a short life once mixed, from 2 to 10 minutes, so be ready before you mix.

3.	It is very difficult to remove once hardened and should last forever.

4.	Epoxies contain serious chemicals and it is important to follow the manufactures instructions.

5.	Most epoxies are waterproof.

PVA Glues
(WeldBond)

This are many brands of PVA glues. You know them as Elmer's, Tacky Glue, etc. The most widely used and preferred by mosaic artists is <u>WeldBond</u>. As I go forward in this section <u>Weldbond</u> is the product that I will be referring to and the one I recommend.

- Non-Toxic, safe for children and fume free.
- Dries clear. Great when bonding transparent and semi transparent materials such as glass to glass.
- May be used as a sealer on porous bases like wood and terra cotta. Mix 5 parts water to 1 part <u>Weldbond</u>. Paint the surface with this mixture and allow to dry.
- Bonds to most anything. Glass, marble, terra Cotta, wood, Formica, etc. It is always beneficial to score (rough up) smooth surfaces to give them a little tooth. This process creates a better bond when using most all types of adhesives. You can scratch them up with a sharp object or sand with a course grade of sandpaper.
- Cleans up with water while it is still in it's "white" stage.
- High temperatures and low humidity will speed the curing process. Cure is complete once it has turned clear. It will continue to strengthen over time.
- Works well to adhere tesserae to mosaic mesh when using the mesh method.
- It can be applied directly from the bottle. My preferred method of application is to work from a small snap lid container and paint it on with a small paint brush. This allows the glue to tack up a bit while in a open container.
- When using to adhere glass to glass the lack of exposure to air will lengthen the dry time and the larger the pieces that you are gluing the longer it will take to cure clear.
- Read the manufactures instructions! For further info about <u>Weldbond</u> that are not answered here, see the manufacturers specifications available at <u>Frank T. Ross</u>.

Adhesive info from witsendmosaic.com

Thinset

Thinset is a cement based adhesive you mix with water OR an liquid polymer additive for added flexibility and durability. Note: Some thinsets already have an additive and should be mixed with water. Check the manufactures recommendations. Thinset is totally waterproof and is the perfect choice for all projects that will be exposed to moisture.

- Read the bag! There is a wealth of information included and products vary.
- Thinset is a cement based adhesive. It does not dry. It is a chemical process that cures. The longer this process takes the stronger the thinset will be. The basic ingredients in thinset are Portland cement, sand, and water, once mixed together a chemical hardening process begins. It will even harden underwater.
- ALWAYS where a dust mask or respirator while exposed to thinset is in it's powdered state. Once mixed with water it is safe to remove. Here why, once inhaled the thinset comes in contact with your respiratory system which is full of moisture. The moisture (water) is the last ingredient that the thinset needs to start getting hard and you don't want lungs full of hard cement!
- DO NOT empty or clean your tools into the sink or drain. Remember thinset will harden under water and in your pipes! The only person who will be happy about that is the plumber! I use a slop bucket to clean up. Once the water is to "icky" I pour off the top liquid in a corner of my garden and allow the rest to dry out. Then you can just bang out the contents of the bucket in the garbage.
- DO NOT add water once the mixture has set more than 5 minutes. If your thinset is getting to hard to work with mix a new batch, adding more water will make it weak.
- Now that I have you wondering why you would ever use it. I have to tell you thinset is always my adhesive of choice for exterior applications and most interior installations unless I am working on a backing that requires a clear or flexible adhesive. It works and it's permanent!
- My best thinset tip - I mix my thinset in an old sour cream containers. That way I don't have to clean it up I can just toss it. Once mixed I place the thinset in a sandwich size Ziploc bag. You can then nip off the corner and apply it to your surface like using a cake decorating bag, just spread with a palette knife.
- Thinset is your best choice if your base is concrete, terra cotta, cement backer boards, Wedi board and most permanent installations.
- It is the only adhesive you can use to really 'float' tiles. This means you can build up the adhesive under a thinner piece of tile so that it is flush with the thick tile next to it.
- Available in white or gray. Typically use white if your planning light grout and gray with dark. Note that the color of the thinset can effect semi translucent tesserae.
- To extend the cure time place a damp towel over your project to prevent it from drying out to quickly. As an added precaution you can cover with a garbage bag.
- It is best to seal cement, brick, terra cotta and other porous surface before applying thinset. These materials will wick (draw) the moisture out of the thinset to quickly and weaken it. You can use Weldbond, or commercial bonding primers.

Gently spiralling bands of mosaic look very effective on a tall, elegantly shaped vase. The top and base of the vase are given a marble finish to enclose the rest of the mosaic.

Spiral Vase

You will need

Tall vase

Yacht varnish and paintbrush (optional)

White chalk

Marble tile

Piece of sacking (heavy cloth)

Hammer

Tile adhesive

Flexible knife

Glazed ceramic household tiles:

pale blue and royal blue

Gold smalti

Tile nippers

Notched spreader or cloth pad

Sponge

Abrasive paper (sandpaper)

Soft cloth

1 If your vase is unglazed, seal it by painting all around the inside top lip with yacht varnish. Using a piece of white chalk, draw lines spiralling gently from the rim of the vase to the base. Make sure you have an even number of bands and that they are regularly spaced.

2 Wrap the marble tile in sacking (heavy cloth), then break it up using a hammer. Using a flexible knife, spread a thin band of tile adhesive around the top and bottom of the vase, press in the marble pieces and leave to dry overnight.

3 Using a hammer and a piece of sacking, break up all the pale blue and royal blue tiles. Spread tile adhesive over the vase, a band at a time, and press in the tesserae, alternating the two colours. Leave to dry, preferably overnight.

4 Use the tile nippers to cut the gold smalti into small pieces. Using the flexible knife, place blobs of adhesive in the larger gaps between the blue tesserae. Press the gold smalti pieces at random over the blue spirals, checking that they are all level with the rest of the tiles. Leave to dry overnight.

5 Using a notched spreader or cloth pad, rub more tile adhesive in the colour of your choice over the surface of the mosaic, carefully filling all the gaps. Wipe off the excess with a damp sponge and leave to dry overnight. Sand off any adhesive dried on the surface, then polish with a dry, soft cloth.

In this unusual modern design, the coloured grout forms a major feature, with untiled areas left to show it off. Within this design, the tesserae appear as separate decorative elements, rather than parts of a whole.

Funky Fruit Bowl

You will need
Soft dark pencil
Terracotta bowl
Vitreous glass mosaic tiles: yellow,
turquoise and white
Tile nippers
PVA (white) glue
Paintbrush
White glazed ceramic household tiles
Matt (flat) coloured glass nuggets
Fabric stain
Flexible knife
Tile grout
Rubber spreader
Sponge
Soft cloth

1 Using a soft pencil, draw freehand spirals on the outside of the bowl, as shown. Each spiral should be about the same depth as the pot. Mark a row of triangles along the edges of each spiral.

2 Using tile nippers, cut the glass tiles into small, equal-sized triangles, to fit the triangles drawn on the bowl.

3 Place a small blob of PVA (white) glue on each pencilled triangle, then press on a glass triangle. Hold the tesserae in place until they stick.

4 Using tile nippers, cut the white ceramic tiles into large triangles of equal size.

▶

5 Apply a thick layer of glue over the inside of the bowl and over the back of each triangle. Press the triangles in place, leaving large gaps between them.

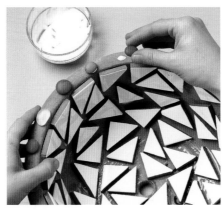

6 Dot blobs of glue at regular intervals around the rim of the bowl and press in the glass nuggets. Leave to dry overnight.

7 Mix the fabric stain with water. You can choose any of the many colours available. Bright primary colours will work well with this design.

8 Gradually add the stain to the tile grout, a spoonful at a time, and mix thoroughly. The final colour of the grout once it has dried will be slightly lighter than its colour when wet.

9 Using a rubber spreader, spread the coloured grout over the entire bowl, evening out the surface. Gently smooth it all over the bowl with your hands. Wipe off the excess grout with a damp sponge. Leave to dry for 1 hour.

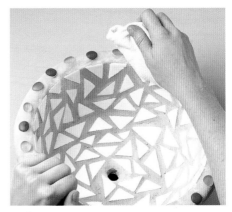

10 Polish the surface of the bowl with a dry, soft cloth, removing any residual tile grout.

In this lovely hallway mirror, romantic red hearts and scrolling white lines are beautifully set off by the rich blue background, which sparkles from the inset chunks of mirror glass.

Valentine Mirror

You will need

12mm (½in) thick plywood sheet, to size of mirror frame required

PVA (white) glue

Paintbrush

Bradawl

Drill and rebate (rabbet) bit

Mirror plate, with keyhole opening

Screwdriver

2 x 12mm (½in) screws

Mirror

Brown paper

Scissors

Masking tape

Ruler

Soft dark pencil

Tile adhesive

Thin-glazed ceramic household tiles: red, white and several rich shades of blue

Tile nippers

Flexible knife

Hammer

Mirror tiles

Piece of sacking (heavy cloth)

Notched spreader

Rubber spreader

Fine abrasive paper (sandpaper)

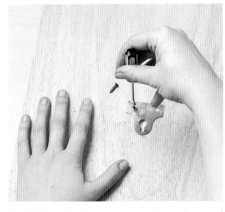

1 Prime both sides of the plywood with diluted PVA (white) glue and leave to dry. Score one side (the front) with a bradawl. Turn the board over and make a dent in the centre about a third of the way down, using a drill. Screw the mirror plate over the dent.

2 Cut a piece of brown paper to the size of the mirror and tape it around the edge to protect the glass. Mark its position in the centre front of the plywood board with a ruler and pencil, and stick it in place with tile adhesive.

3 Draw a small heart in the centre of each border and scrolling lines to connect the four hearts.

4 Using tile nippers, cut the red tiles into small, irregular pieces and the white tiles into regular-sized squares.

5 Spread the tile adhesive over the pencilled heart shapes with a flexible knife and press in the red tile pieces. Repeat for the scroll lines using the white tiles. Scrape off any excess adhesive and leave to dry overnight.

6 Using a hammer, carefully break up the blue ceramic tiles and the mirror tiles into small pieces. It is advisable to wrap each tile in a piece of sacking (heavy cloth) before breaking up, to avoid the tile shattering or splintering.

7 Working on a small area at a time, spread tile adhesive over the background areas with a notched spreader, then press in the blue and mirror pieces. Leave to dry overnight.

8 Grout the mosaic with tile adhesive, using a rubber spreader to distribute the adhesive over the flat surface and your fingers for the edges.

9 Carefully sand off any lumps of remaining adhesive that may have dried on the surface of the mosaic, using fine abrasive paper (sandpaper).

10 For a professional finish, rub tile adhesive into the back of the plywood board. Remove the protective brown paper from the mirror.

In this vivid mosaic, it is important that the tesserae are accurately shaped, with no gaps between them. They are left ungrouted so that tile adhesive dust will not disturb the workings of the clock.

Cosmic Clock

You will need

40cm (16in) diameter circle of wood

Strip of plywood, 5mm (¹/₁₆in) deeper than the circle of wood and 130cm (52in) long

Hammer

Tacks

Black paint

Paintbrush

Brown paper

Scissors

Drill

Charcoal or black felt-tipped pen

Vitreous glass mosaic tiles

PVA (white) glue and brush

Tile nippers

Tile adhesive

Admix

Grout spreader

Piece of flat wood

Sponge

Craft (utility) knife

Soft cloth

Double-sided tape

Clock mechanism and hands

Picture-hanging hook

1 Position the strip of plywood around the circumference of the circle of wood, and, using a hammer and tacks, cover the edge of the circle to make a neat rim. Paint the rim black and leave to dry. Cut a circle of brown paper to fit inside the rim. Fold it in quarters to find the centre, and make a small hole.

2 Place the paper over the circle of wood and mark the centre through the hole on to the wood. Remove the paper and then drill a hole through the centre of the wood, large enough to allow the spindle of the clock mechanism to rotate freely.

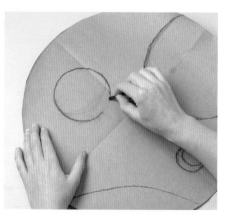

3 Draw a cosmic design on the brown paper circle, using a stick of charcoal or a felt-tipped pen. (Charcoal is easier to correct.)

4 Snip the glass tiles into tesserae using tile nippers, then stick the tesserae face down on the paper, using PVA (white) glue. Place them as close together as possible, without any gaps in between. Make any further cuts necessary to allow them to fit around the curves in your design.

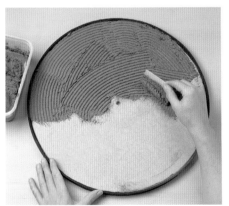

5 Mix the tile adhesive and admix according to the manufacturer's instructions. Using the fine-notched edge of a grout spreader, spread this over the whole of the board, right up to the edge. Lower the mosaic on to the adhesive and press flat.

6 Smooth over the paper with a flat piece of wood, using small, circular movements. Leave for 20 minutes, then dampen the paper and gently pull it away from the mosaic. Scrape away any adhesive that has come through the tesserae with a craft (utility) knife. Leave to dry for at least 2 hours.

7 Carefully wipe any remaining glue from the surface of the mosaic with the sponge and polish with a dry, soft cloth. Using double-sided tape, attach the clock mechanism to the back of the board. Insert the spindle through the hole in the centre and fit on the hands. Fit a picture hook to the back.

This geometric mosaic uses contrasting colours of glass and ceramic tiles to create a stunning wall panel. Mirror and gold-leaf tiles add an opulent feel. Hang this mosaic where it can be a dramatic focal point.

Mirror Mosaic

You will need

Pencil

Ruler

9mm (⅜in) thick MDF (medium-density fiberboard), cut to 46 x 46cm (18 x 18in)

Paintbrushes

PVA (white) glue

Tile adhesive

Mirror, cut to 19.5 x 19.5cm (7¾ x 7¾in)

Gold vitreous glass tiles in a light and dark shade

Matt (flat) ceramic mosaic tiles in light and dark shades

Tile nippers

Mirror tiles

Tile grout

Rubber spreader

Sponge

Soft cloth

1 Using a pencil and ruler, divide the board so that there are seven equal spaces along each edge. Join up your marks carefully to form a grid of squares. Mark the alternate squares with a pencil squiggle to show where the different squares of tones will be mosaiced.

2 Using a large paintbrush, seal the board with a coat of PVA (white) glue diluted 1:1 with water. Allow to dry thoroughly. The PVA will dry clear, so the design will still be visible.

3 Using tile adhesive, stick the main mirror on to the centre of the board so that there are even borders all around it. Leave it to dry.

4 Cut the gold vitreous glass and the two shades of ceramic mosaic tiles in half with the tile nippers. Squeeze the nippers firmly for a clean cut.

▶

5 Starting on the squares marked with the pencil squiggles, stick the tiles in position, alternating between a light shade of vitreous glass and a light shade of matt (flat) ceramic. Leave a slight gap between each piece. Paint undiluted PVA glue on to each square and stick the tiles to fit within the pencil guidelines.

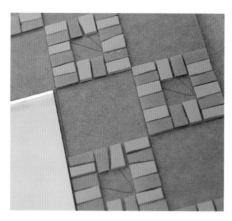

6 Finish sticking these lighter squares over the entire board, working carefully to ensure the gaps between each piece remain even.

7 Cover the alternate squares over the entire board with two darker colours, one of the matt ceramic, and the other of the vitreous glass, sticking them in position as before and keeping the spacing even throughout.

8 Stick the mirror tiles in the centre of the darker squares using PVA glue as before to create a dark square with a centre of light.

9 Stick squares of the darker vitreous glass tiles in the centre of the lighter squares to create lighter squares with a dark centre. Allow to dry.

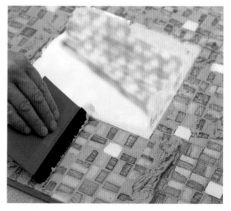

10 Spread tile grout evenly over the board with a rubber spreader, making sure the gaps between the tiles have been filled. Smooth a little grout around the edge of the board. With a slightly damp sponge, wipe away any excess grout from the surface and the edge of the board. Leave to dry. Polish with a dry, soft cloth.

A simple spiral was the inspiration for this tall, elegant lamp base. Pieces of mirror have been added to catch the light, and they sparkle when the lamp is switched on.

Spiral Lamp Stand

You will need

Cardboard carpet roll tube

5mm (¼in) thick plywood sheet

Pencil

Jigsaw (saber saw)

Drill with a bit just larger than the metal rod

Bradawl or awl

Wood glue

Shellac

Paintbrushes

Lamp power cord

Hollow metal rod with a screw thread, cut to the height required

Plaster of Paris

Ceramic household tiles in three colours

Tile nippers

Tile adhesive

Sponge

Mirror

Flexible knife

Abasive paper (sandpaper)

Soft cloth

Copper pipe

Hacksaw

Lamp fittings

Plug

Screwdriver

Lampshade

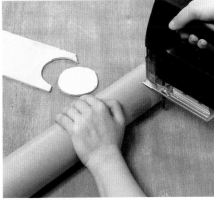

1 Draw twice around the circular end of the cardboard tube on to the plywood. Cut around these circles using a jigsaw (saber saw) and cut the cardboard tube to the length required. Drill a hole through the centre of one of the plywood circles. Use a bradawl to make a hole in the cardboard tube 2cm (¾in) in from one end and large enough to take the lamp power cord.

2 Use wood glue to stick the plywood circle without the drilled hole to the end of the tube near the cord hole. Leave to dry overnight, then paint the cardboard tube with shellac. Thread the cord in through the hole in the tube and then through the hollow metal rod. Stand the metal rod inside the tube with the screw thread at the top.

3 Mix some plaster of Paris with water and quickly pour it into the tube. Slip the second plywood circle over the metal rod and secure it with wood glue to the top of the cardboard tube. As soon as you have poured the plaster of Paris into the tube, you must work quickly to secure the top, as it is very important that the plaster dries with the rod in an upright position.

▶

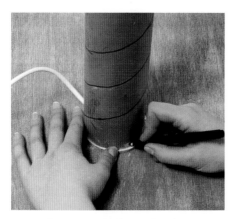

4 With a pencil, draw the design on to the tube, following the spiral lines already present on the cardboard tube. You can add variations and embellishments at this stage.

5 Cut the tiles for the outline colour into small pieces using tile nippers. Stick these to the lines of your design using tile adhesive. Use a sponge to wipe away any large blobs of adhesive that seep out from under the tesserae, then leave to dry overnight.

6 Select two colours of tile to fill the areas between the spiralling lines. Use the tile nippers to cut the tiles into various shapes and sizes, then cut the mirror into various shapes and sizes.

7 Spread tile adhesive on to the remaining cardboard area with a flexible knife, and apply the tesserae in separate bands of colour. Work on a small area at a time, so that the surface does not become too messy. Intersperse the coloured tesserae with pieces of mirror as you work. Cover the whole surface of the cardboard tube, then leave it to dry overnight.

8 Apply more tile adhesive over the whole area of the lamp stand, taking care to press it down between all the tesserae. Wipe off the excess adhesive with a damp sponge and leave the stand to dry overnight. Rub off any excess surface adhesive with abrasive paper (sandpaper), and polish with a dry, soft cloth.

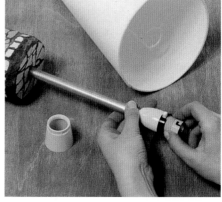

9 Finish off by attaching all the fittings. Slip the copper pipe, cut to size, over the central rod, leaving the screw end exposed. Attach the lamp fittings, plug and lampshade.

This candle sconce looks beautiful hung on a bathroom wall or in a bedroom. The mirror reflects the candlelight and, together with the small pieces of coloured tile, this gives the mosaic a magical quality.

Candle Sconce

You will need

Tape measure

2cm (³⁄₄in) thick plywood sheet

Pencil

Ruler

Vitreous glass mosaic tiles

Jigsaw (saber saw)

Abrasive paper (sandpaper)

Wire cutters

Chicken wire

Hammer

U-shaped nails

Picture hooks

Bonding plaster

PVA (white) glue

Sponge

Tile adhesive

Knife

Vitreous glass mosaic tiles, mirror, washed glass, stained glass, and amethyst

Tile nippers

Craft (utility) knife

Tile grout

Soft cloths

Old sheet

Drill with rebate (rabbet) bit

Mirror plate, with keyhole opening

Screwgun or screwdriver

Small screws

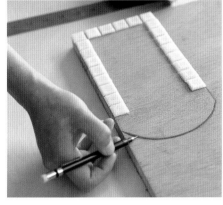

1 Measure and mark out the plywood to a width to fit six whole glass tiles (13cm/5¼in) and length to fit 10 whole tiles (22cm/9in). Use a ruler, working from the corner of the wood and the two straight edges. At the end of this rectangle, draw a semicircle.

2 Clamp the wood on to the edge of a workbench. Using a jigsaw (saber saw), cut out the shape. Sand the edges of the wood lightly.

3 Using wire cutters, cut out a piece of chicken wire 20 x 50cm (8 x 20in). With a hammer and U-shaped nails, attach one end of the wire to the semi-circle to create a curve. Remove the excess wire using wire cutters or pliers.

4 Fold the wire over and compress it to create the basic shape, fixing the top end to the wood with picture hooks. Mix up some bonding plaster in a bucket into a soft but firm consistency. Pack this into the chicken wire until the structure is filled. Start to create the shape by applying small lumps where there are uneven dips. ▶

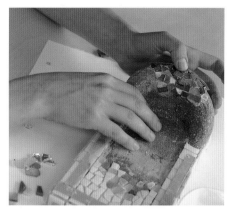

5 When the shape is complete, dip your fingers into water and run them over the surfaces until there is a smooth finish. Leave the plaster to dry for 24 hours, then seal the surface with a thin film of diluted PVA (white) glue, applied with a sponge.

6 Using a knife, apply an even layer of tile adhesive to the outer edges, or border, of the candle sconce. Stick strips of whole vitreous glass tiles (paper side up) on to the border, clipping the last tile to fit and meet the curve at the top of the sculptured holder. Stick further strips of glass tiles on to the sides of the sconce, continuing around the base. Clip the remaining glass tiles and all the other tiles into small pieces.

7 Starting from the top, within the border created from whole tiles, apply tile adhesive and place small, clipped pieces of white tile next to the whole tiles. As the space fills, introduce light pieces of pale blue and green washed glass, working downwards. On the shaped holder, work with richer greens and blues, and include pieces of stained glass and amethyst. Place pieces of mirror randomly to reflect the light.

8 When the mosaic is finished, remove the brown paper on the whole tiles, having moistened it with a damp sponge. Clean the surfaces of the tiles and remove any excess adhesive in the gaps with a craft (utility) knife.

9 Apply tile grout over the mosaic, working it into the gaps with your fingers. Gently clean off any excess grout with a damp sponge. After about 10 minutes, use a dry cloth to rub away any excess grout. If it is still wet, leave it for a little while then try again.

10 Place the completed candle sconce face down on an old sheet. Place the mirror plate in position, then mark with a pencil the area under the keyhole-shaped opening. Drill this area so that it is large enough to take a screw head, then screw the mirror plate in position.

A breezeblock makes a safe, solid base for a large lamp. It is covered in a chunky floral design made of floor tiles and marble, with tiny pieces of mirror set into the gaps to catch the light from the lamp.

Floral Lamp Base

You will need

Breezeblock (cinderblock)

Ruler

Soft pencil

Drill with a long bit (at least half the length of the block and just wider than the metal rod)

Chisel

Hammer

Lamp power cord

Hollow metal rod with a screw thread, cut to the height required for the lamp

Tile adhesive

Piece of chalk

Ceramic floor tiles: shades of yellow for the petals

Piece of sacking (heavy cloth)

Flexible knife

White marble tiles

Mirror

Tile nippers

Rubber spreader

Sponge

Dust mask

Abrasive paper (sandpaper)

Soft cloth

Copper pipe

Hacksaw

Lamp fittings

Plug

Screwdriver

Lampshade

1 On one end of the breezeblock (cinderblock), mark diagonal lines to find the centre. Drill a hole right through, turning the block over if necessary to drill from the other end.

2 On one end, use a chisel to cut a deep groove from the centre hole to one edge to contain the lamp power cord. This will be the bottom of the lamp base.

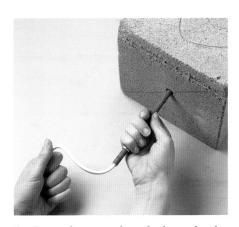

3 Pass the metal rod through the centre hole, with the screw thread at the top, then thread the cord through the rod, leaving a long length at the bottom. Tuck the cord into its groove, leaving enough length to reach an electrical socket. Fill in the groove with tile adhesive to secure the flex. Leave to dry.

4 Using a piece of chalk, draw a large, simple flower design on the sides of the breezeblock. Exclude the bottom of the block. Plan out the colour scheme for your petals, keeping the yellow for the flower centres and white for the background.

▶

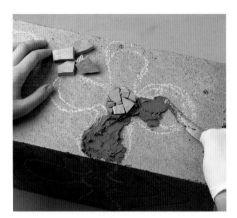

5 Wrap each floor tile in sacking (heavy cloth) and break it up into pieces with a hammer. Using a flexible knife, spread tile adhesive over each flower shape. Press the yellow tesserae into the adhesive and build up the flower centres. Now start work on the petals, using the other tiles, and continue until they are all covered.

6 Break up each white marble tile in the same way. Working on a small area at a time, spread tile adhesive over the background and press in the marble pieces. Don't worry if your pieces don't butt up to each other. Leave to dry for 12 hours or overnight.

7 Using tile nippers, cut the mirror into small fragments. Insert blobs of tile adhesive into the larger gaps between the tesserae. Then push in the mirror fragments, checking they are level with the rest. Continue inserting mirrored pieces over the base until covered. Leave to dry overnight.

8 Grout the lamp base by scraping tile adhesive over the surface with a rubber spreader. This will bind all the pieces of tesserae together firmly. Use your fingers to smooth it right into the fissures and along the sides of the block. Wipe off the excess tile adhesive with a damp sponge and leave to dry overnight.

9 Wearing a dust mask, sand off any adhesive that may have dried on the surface. Polish with a soft, dry cloth. Finish off by slipping the copper pipe, cut to size, over the hollow rod, so that the screw end is exposed. Attach the lamp fittings, bulb, plug and chosen lampshade.

In this project, vitreous glass mosaic tiles in striking colours are used to decorate a ready-made fire screen. Most of this design uses whole tiles, cut diagonally into triangles.

Mosaic Fire Screen

You will need

Ready-made fire-screen base

Pencil

Ruler

Craft (utility) knife

PVA (white) glue

Paintbrushes

Vitreous glass mosaic tiles

Tile nippers

Tile grout

Nailbrush

Wood primer

White undercoat paint

Gloss paint

Soft cloth

1 Draw the design on to the surface of the screen and its feet. Calculate the space needed to accommodate the tiles required and mark the main areas with a ruler. Score the whole of the surface with a craft (utility) knife, then prime with diluted PVA (white) glue and leave to dry completely.

2 Select a range of vitreous glass tiles in the colours you require. Use tile nippers to cut some of the tiles into right-angled triangles for use in the inner border design.

3 Stick the tiles and half-tiles to the base with undiluted PVA glue. Try to make all the gaps between the tiles equal and leave the area that will be slotted into the feet untiled.

4 Tile the edge, then the feet, making sure that they will still slot on to the screen. Leave overnight to dry. Rub tile grout into the entire surface of the mosaic with your fingers, making sure that all the gaps between the tesserae are filled.

5 Leave the grout to dry for about 10 minutes, then remove any excess with a nailbrush. Allow to dry for a further 12 hours, then paint the back of the screen with wood primer, then undercoat paint and finally gloss paint, allowing each coat to dry before you apply the next. Finally, polish the mosaic with a dry, soft cloth and slot on the feet.

This abstract frame, with its glowing colours, was created using the semi-indirect method of mosaics. In this way, you can arrange the tesserae on paper first, before committing yourself to the final design.

Abstract Mirror

You will need

40cm (16in) diameter circle of wood

Brown paper

Pair of compasses

Pencil

Scissors

20cm (8in) diameter circle of mirror

Black felt-tipped pen

Masking tape

Vitreous glass mosaic tiles

Tile nippers

PVA (white) glue and brush

Strip of plywood, 5mm (¼in) deeper than the circle of wood and 130cm (52in) long, painted black

Hammer

Tacks

Craft (utility) knife

Tile grout

Sponge

Tile adhesive

Grout spreader

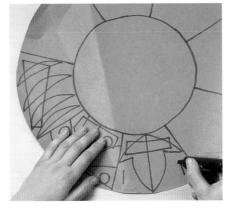

1 Using a pair of compasses, draw a circle on brown paper 2mm (¹⁄₁₆in) smaller than the wooden circle. Cut it out. Place the mirror in the centre and draw around it in black pen. Divide the border into eight equal sections. Draw a design clearly in each section.

2 Place the mirror face down in the centre of the paper and attach it from underneath with masking tape.

3 Cut the tiles into tesserae of the right size with tile nippers. Stick them face down on the paper design, using PVA (white) glue. Keep the gaps between them as even as possible.

4 When the design is complete, carefully lower the mosaic on to the board. Position the strip of plywood around the edge of the circle and attach it using a hammer and tacks to form a rim. Remove the mirror and cut away the brown paper underneath, using a craft (utility) knife.

▶

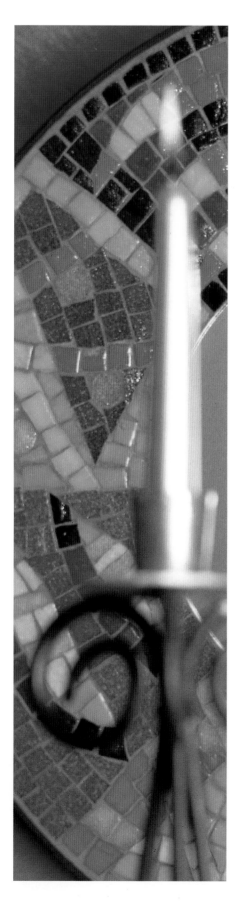

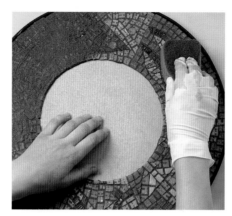

5 Rub a small amount of tile grout into the mosaic with your fingers, then wipe off the excess with a damp sponge. This will bind the tesserae together. Leave until almost dry.

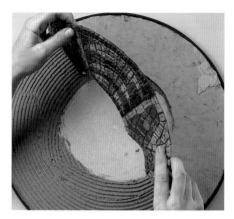

6 Gently remove the mosaic from the board by turning it upside down. Using the fine-notched side of a grout spreader, spread the outer area of the board with tile adhesive. Lower the mosaic down into the adhesive, mosaic side down, and press firmly.

7 Coat the back of the mirror with tile adhesive and stick it in the centre. Leave to set for 20 minutes.

8 Dampen the paper with a wet sponge, wait for 10 minutes until the glue has dissolved, then gently peel it off the mosaic. Clean away any protruding lumps of adhesive with a damp sponge. Leave to dry, then re-grout, filling in any cracks, and sponge clean.

Mosaic forms a very effective surround to a mirror: the undulating, fractured surface perfectly sets off the smooth, reflective plane of the glass, used here with china, delicate patterns and touches of gold.

Bathroom Mirror

You will need

2cm (¾in) thick plywood sheet, cut to size required

Pencil

Ruler

Jigsaw (saber saw)

Abrasive paper (sandpaper)

PVA (white) glue

Paintbrushes

Wood primer

White undercoat paint

Gloss paint

Drill with rebate (rabbet) bit

Mirror plate, with keyhole opening

2 x 2cm (¾in) screws

Screwdriver

Thick card (stock)

3mm (⅛in) thick foil-backed mirror

Tile adhesive

Flexible knife

Masking tape

Tracing paper (optional)

Selection of china

Tile nippers

Tile grout

Vinyl matt emulsion (flat latex) or acrylic paint (optional)

Rubber spreader

Nailbrush

Soft cloth

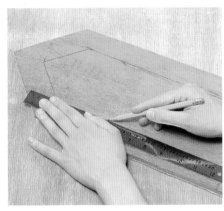

1 Draw the outer shape of the mirror frame on to the piece of plywood. Cut around this shape using a jigsaw (saber saw), then sand down the rough edges. On to this base panel, draw the desired shape of the mirror. Here, the shape of the mirror echoes the shape of the panel, but it could be a completely different shape if desired. Make sure it is a shape that the glass supplier will be able to reproduce.

3 Make a card (stock) template in the exact dimensions of the mirror shape you have drawn on the base. Ask your supplier to cut a piece of 3mm (⅛in) foil-backed mirror using the template.

2 Seal the sides and front of the base panel with diluted PVA (white) glue, and paint the back, first with wood primer, then undercoat paint and finally gloss paint. Mark the position of the mirror plate on the back of the panel. Using a rebate (rabbet) bit, drill the area that will be under the key-hole-shaped opening so that it is large enough to take a screw head, then screw the mirror plate in position.

4 Stick the mirror in position using tile adhesive spread with a flexible knife. Leave to dry overnight.

▶

5 Trim 2mm (¹⁄₁₆in) from the card template all around the edge and cover the mirror with it, securing it in place with masking tape; this should prevent the mirror from being scratched or covered with adhesive. The mosaic will eventually overlap this 2mm (¹⁄₁₆in) of uncovered mirror.

6 Draw the design for the frame on the dry, sealed surface surrounding the mirror; use tracing paper and a soft pencil to copy and transfer your original plan, if you wish.

7 Using tile nippers, snip the smooth edges from the cups and plates you have collected. Use these to tile the outside edge of the base panel and to overlap the 2mm (¹⁄₁₆in) edges of the mirror, sticking them down with tile adhesive. Cut the remainder of the china into small pieces and stick these along the structural lines of your design.

8 Fill in the areas of detail between the outlining tesserae. When the mirror frame is completely tiled, leave to dry for 24 hours.

9 Mix tile grout with vinyl matt emulsion (flat latex) or acrylic paint, if colour is desired. Spread this over the surface of the tesserae using a rubber spreader, and rub it in by hand, making sure all the gaps are filled. Allow the surface to dry for 10 minutes, then brush off the excess grout with a stiff-bristled nailbrush. Wipe clean with a dry, soft cloth.

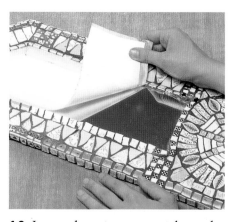

10 Leave the mirror overnight to dry thoroughly, then remove the protective card from the mirror. Finally, hang the mirror in position using the mirror plate on the back of the panel.

This delicate mosaic is made entirely from old cups and plates. The pretty trinket box is ideal for displaying on a dressing table, and can be used for storing jewellery, letters and other treasures.

Floral Trinket Box

You will need
Wooden box
PVA (white) glue
Paintbrush
Bradawl or awl
Soft dark pencil
Selection of china: white and patterned
Tile nippers
Tile adhesive
Admix
Flexible knife
Sponge
Paint scraper
Soft cloth

1 Prime the top and sides of the wooden box with diluted PVA (white) glue. Leave to dry, then score at random with a bradawl or awl to provide a good key.

2 Using a soft pencil, draw a grid on the box. Freehand, draw a flower in each square, and a large flower in the centre. Keep the design simple for the best effect.

3 Using tile nippers, cut white pieces of china into small squares. Mix the tile adhesive with admix following the manufacturer's instructions. Using a flexible knife, spread this along the grid lines, a small area at a time.

4 Press the white tesserae into the adhesive in neat, close-fitting rows. Cover all the grid lines on both the top and sides of the box. Leave to dry overnight.

▶

5 Using tile nippers, cut out small patterned pieces from the china and sort them into colours. Position the tesserae on the box and plan out the colour scheme for the mosaic before committing to the design.

6 Spread the tile adhesive and admix mixture over each square of the top and sides in turn. Press in the tesserae to make each flower and use a contrasting, plain colour in the background. Leave to dry.

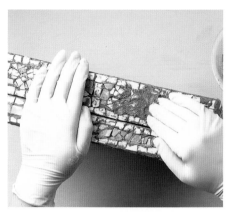

7 Using your fingers, spread tile adhesive all over the surface of the mosaic, getting right into the crevices. Wipe off any excess adhesive with a damp cloth or sponge.

8 Using a flexible knife, smooth the tile adhesive around the hinges and clasp, if there is one. Remove any excess adhesive immediately with a sponge before it dries. Leave to dry.

9 Carefully scrape off any tile adhesive that may have dried on the surface of the mosaic with a paint scraper. Take care not to scratch the surface of the tiles.

10 When all the excess grout has been removed, polish the surface of the box with a dry, soft cloth, rubbing each tile fragment to a high shine.

In this piece, mosaic adds intense colour, and a contrasting effect, to a three-dimensional object. The colours and laying techniques convey an intensity of expression as well as a striking aesthetic effect.

Sculptural Head

You will need

Plaster head

Fine aluminium mesh

Wire

Tile adhesive

Small plasterer's trowel

Vitreous glass mosaic tiles in various colours

Tile nippers

Black tile grout

Tiler's sponge

Small screwdriver

Fine wet-and-dry (silicon carbide) paper

Soft cloth

1 In this example, the base has been made from an original plaster head. Press a fine aluminium mesh against the surface of a plaster head and fold and mould it carefully to create the contours of the face and head. Do this in two halves, from the front around the contours of the face, and from the back, then remove them and join them together with twists of wire.

2 Create the form by applying a 12mm (½in) thick layer of tile adhesive over the mesh head with a small plasterer's trowel. Apply a thin layer first and work into the surface of the mesh, followed immediately (that is before it dries out) with a thicker layer. Some further modelling can be done at this stage, using the build-up of adhesive to refine the contours.

3 Cover the head in quarter-cut vitreous glass tesserae, sticking them to the base with a thin layer of tile adhesive. Apply this to small areas at a time with a small plasterer's trowel. The eyebrows would be a good place to start, as their curving lines generate the undulating lines of the forehead.

4 The eyes are very important in giving the piece definition and character and need to be tackled early in the process, as they will generate the laying lines of the cheeks. To maintain the even flow of mosaic, try to use full-quarter tiles where possible and avoid resorting to very small pieces, which will look clumsy and can be difficult to fix firmly.

▶

5 Where you are forming a sudden change in plane, such as over the eyebrows, around the top of the crown and at the edge of the ears, try to fix the pieces so that one bevelled edge joins up to another. This will keep the joint width as narrow as possible. These pieces will slightly overhang the base, and it is important to use enough adhesive to bond them firmly.

6 The lines of mosaic around the circumference of the neck have been carefully merged with the lines across the cheeks. Junctions of smaller cut tiles can be made where the line created relates to the form, such as around the eye socket and abutting the ear, but where the form requires a more gradual transition a blending of the lines will be less distracting and neater.

7 Cover the neck and face in a series of three-colour mixes that blend into each other by carrying one colour over into the next mix and avoiding harsh dividing lines. Lay the hair, crown and dress in two-colour stripes; the more organized patterns help to suggest a different texture from the areas of "skin". Make a contrast between the uniform treatment of the dress and crown across the piece and the asymmetry of the face and hair.

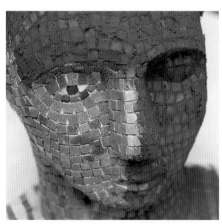

8 When the piece is covered and the adhesive is dry, apply black tile grout. Work the grout into the joints, curves and awkward corners with your fingers. Black grout gives extra intensity to the colours.

9 While the grout is still wet, wipe it clean using a densely textured tiler's sponge. Rinse the sponge often and avoid passing a dirty side back over the mosaic, as this will spread the grout rather than remove it. In fiddly areas, you may need to scrape away excess grout with a small screwdriver. Rub down any sharp edges with fine wet-and-dry (silicon carbide) paper, then leave to dry. Finally, polish the piece with a dry, soft cloth.

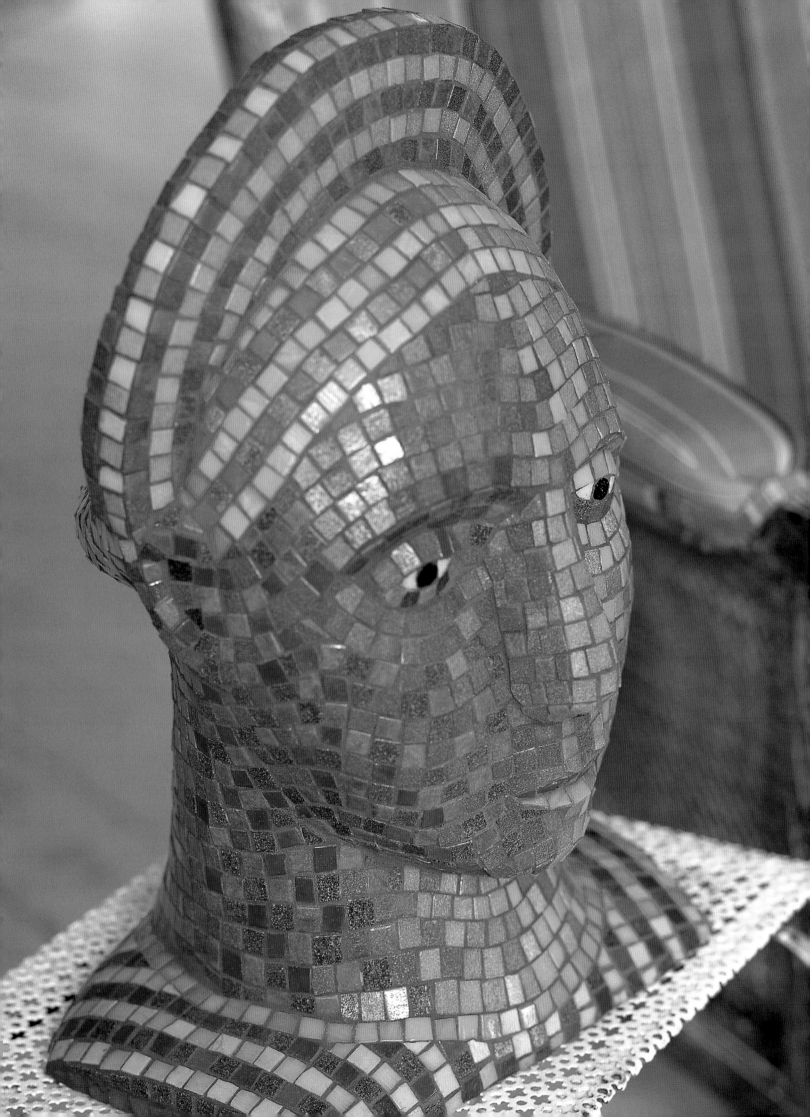

Furniture

In this chapter there are plenty of ideas for creating and redecorating pieces of furniture, old or new. Revamp an old chest of drawers, or give a new lease of life to an ageing bedhead. The designs here are just the beginning – every project will have a unique angle, and every room is different, so your finished result will be completely original. Use mosaic to customize your furniture with colour and texture.

Almost every room in the house contains an item of furniture that could be personalized by mosaic: from storage chests and chests of drawers to bedheads, home office furniture and screens.

Chests, beds and screens

Bedheads, chests, cupboards and screens are just some of the pieces of furniture that can be transformed by mosaic. Just a quick look around your house will give you plenty of inspiration.

Chests

Mosaic can turn both kinds of chests into highly unusual objects. A chest with a lifting lid can have panels of mosaic applied to the lid and front, while chests of drawers (bureaux) can have small matching or related motifs on each drawer. It is vital with such items that the tesserae do not impede the movement of drawers or doors.

Above: Both end panels and a central panel on the door of this cupboard have been enlivened with mosaics using pieces of old china in a geometric design.

Left: The daisy-filled panels of this pine bedhead would look beautiful in a country-style bedroom.

Cupboards and dressers

Think about adding mosaic to the doors of cupboards or dressers. You do not have to cover the whole door; a small panel with perhaps a decorative border would suffice. Mosaic is an inventive way of reviving and personalizing mass-produced items of furniture or secondhand pieces.

Above: Each drawer of this miniature wooden storage chest has its own striking motif, with just five colours of tiles used in the whole piece.

Left: In this golden stained-glass mosaic screen, the stained glass was laid on top of clear glass so that the light can still shine through. Bands of colour flow freely across the panels, giving a sense of movement.

Mosaic can be heavy, so you need to be sure that the furniture joints and any hinges, as well as the floor, will carry the extra weight. A cupboard with rather weak hinges could have its doors hanging under the extra weight.

When working on wood, a compound called admix may be added to tile adhesive to make it more flexible.

Beds

Wooden bedheads and footboards provide the opportunity for a bedroom transformation. The decorative theme could be carried on to other pieces of furniture in the bedroom, such as a bedside cabinet or chest of drawers, for a matching set.

Instead of the folk art flowers used on the opposite page, you could draw a modern, abstract design and fill it in with bold colours. Consider other themes for different areas of the house: a young child's bed, for example, could have a snakes and ladders design.

Home office

Desks, computer tables, filing cabinets and other home office furniture could benefit from mosaic panels or inserts. Remember that such pieces must do the job for which they are intended: computer tables should form a wobble-free base for the equipment; filing cabinets must have drawers that open and close; and it has to be possible to write

and read easily at a desk. Adding personal touches in the form of mosaics – perhaps incorporating some symbol, logo or initials connected to the business – is a good way of making functional areas less intrusive in the rest of the living space.

Screens

A screen is the perfect solution for dividing a room into different areas, but a touch of lightness is needed to stop it becoming too slab-like. Mirror could be successful, as would gold, silver or other metallic materials in geometric and abstract designs. The play of light, natural or artificial, will add mystery, lightness and movement.

The humble table top is an ideal surface for a mosaicist, being flat and at a convenient height to be seen and admired. There are so many different kinds of table, that every room in the house can have one.

Tables

A chess or games table, side, hall or bedside table, perhaps even a dressing table, would be perfect for mosaic. Garden tables are also ideal.

Finding or making a table

Relatively inexpensive tables are available from junk (curio) shops, and mosaic is an imaginative and fulfilling way of personalizing them.

Alternatively, you could easily make your own table tops from MDF (medium-density fiberboard), plywood or other manufactured boards, creating different shapes and sizes to suit your mosaic design by cutting them out with a jigsaw (saber saw) or circular saw.

The edge of the table can be finished in mosaic or have a stainless-steel rim or similar edging. Any sharp mosaic

edges should be sanded down. You can buy simple metal bases or frames to support the table tops from second-hand stores; alternatively, you could commission one from a blacksmith or craftsperson, or just make your own from blocks of wood.

Table surfaces

You need to make sure that the finished result is smooth and even: people must be able to put drinks and vases on them with no danger of them toppling over or wobbling precariously.

You could mosaic the entire table top or you may prefer to insert a decorative panel into a part of it, often the centre. A mosaic border around the edge would also look attractive. Such panels or borders must be flush or level

Above left: The strong rope design mosaic by Celia Gregory suits the square robustness of this coffee table.

Above: The iridiscent and slightly pearlized stained glass is laid in shapes inset on the table top surface to give a flowing and dynamic feeling.

with (not above or below) the rest of the table top, and this needs to be taken into account at the design stage.

If you want to insert a mosaic panel or border, you will need to calculate what depth the finished work will be, then remove that amount from the depth of the table top and sink the mosaic into the prepared area. You should also use pieces of tile throughout with the same thickness.

Non-porous materials, such as glazed clay, glass or a suitable stone, can be easily wiped dry without becoming stained. If the material you choose is porous, you could cover the entire surface of your design with a protective layer of glass. Ask a specialist to cut this to size.

Table-top designs

Your choice of design is, of course, personal, but it is worth noting that repeated patterns and continuous swirling or abstract designs work particularly well on circular tables. You could try a Celtic knot motif or an Islamic organic design. There are many pattern books available in craft shops to use for inspiration. The late Victorians were great pattern book makers, and in these you will find an abundance of choice for designs.

Above right: This table top by Elizabeth De'Ath is decorated with mosaic mirror, divided into sections and bands to create a distinct pattern.

Above far right: This Roman-influenced table top is cut from matt unglazed tiles to a simple roundel shape.

Right: Celtic designs have a timeless quality that suits both modern and traditional furniture.

Never throw away your favourite china when it gets chipped or broken. Instead, give it another chance to shine as one of the patterns in a table-top mosaic. Unlike in a jigsaw, the pieces don't have to fit.

Mosaic Table Top

You will need

2cm (¾in) thick chipboard (particle board)

Saw

5 x 2.5cm (2 x 1in) wood for frame

Mitre saw

Wood glue

Panel pins (brads)

Hammer

Hardboard or thick card (stock)

Metal ruler

Craft (utility) knife

Self-healing cutting mat

PVA (white) glue

Paintbrushes

Old china and clay pots

Old towels

Tile adhesive

Grout spreader

Tile grout

Sponge

Soft cloth

Paint

Polyurethane varnish (optional)

1 Cut the chipboard (particle board) to make a base of the required size for a table. Mitre the length of wood to make a frame to surround the base. Glue and pin the frame. There must be a recess of about 5cm (2in) depending on the depth of the material you are using for the mosaic.

2 Cut a matching piece of thick card (stock) or hardboard to use for planning the design. Use a metal rule and a craft (utility) knife, being careful to press down onto a cut-resistant surface like a cutting mat.

3 Paint the chipboard with diluted PVA (white) glue, to seal the base.

4 Place large pieces of china and pieces of clay pot between two old towels.

▶

5 Smash the china and clay pot with a hammer. This can be done in a controlled way to get the shapes you need and to protect your eyes.

6 Plan the layout of your design on the hardboard or card (stock). The design can be whatever you want: random, geometric or representational.

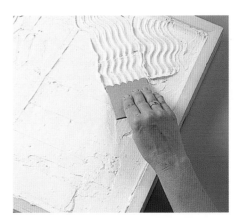

7 Using the notched side of a grout spreader coat the board with a layer of tile adhesive 5mm (¼in) deep. This spreader was made out of thick card.

8 Transfer all the pieces, bedding them down in the adhesive to hide the different thicknesses and to make the surface as level as you can.

9 Leave to dry overnight, then apply the tile grout with a grout spreader. Ensure the grout is evenly distributed between the mosaic pieces.

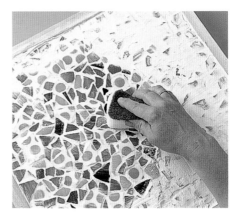

10 When the grout begins to dry, wipe off the excess with a damp sponge.

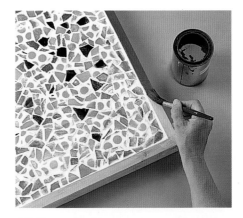

11 When the grout is dry, use a dry, soft cloth to buff up the shiny ceramic surface, so revealing all the colours.

12 Paint the frame, using a colour that complements the mosaic, and apply two coats of polyurethane varnish if it is for outdoor use.

A panelled piece of furniture is ideal for mosaic because it gives you a ready-made frame in which to work. This simple, geometric design is made with pieces of old china and is particularly effective.

Decorative Panel

You will need

Piece of wooden furniture with a framed panel or panels

White spirit (paint thinner)

PVA (white) glue

Paintbrushes

Bradawl or awl

Soft dark pencil

Masking tape

Old china

Tile nippers

Tile adhesive

Admix

Flexible knife

Cloths

Abrasive paper (sandpaper)

Paintscraper

1 Remove any varnish from the areas of wood you wish to mosaic with white spirit (paint thinner). Prime with diluted PVA (white) glue and leave to dry. Score the surface with a bradawl or awl.

2 Draw a simple design on to the wood for the first panel. In this project we started with the cupboard door.

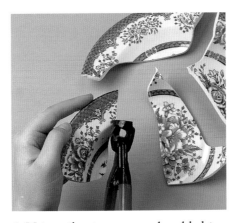

3 Stick masking tape around the raised edges of the panel(s) to protect the surrounding wood.

4 Using tile nippers, cut the old china into small, random shapes. Sort the pieces into colours or shades of particular colours. Test out the colour scheme by positioning the pieces on the design until you are satisfied.

5 Mix the tile adhesive with admix according to the manufacturer's instructions. Working on a small area at a time, spread the mixture over each area of the pencil design with a flexible knife and press on the tesserae. Leave to dry.

▶

6 Grout the mosaic with more tile adhesive and admix mixture. The china pieces will make an uneven surface, so use a piece of cloth to reach into all the gaps. Wipe off the excess then leave to dry overnight.

7 Carefully sand off any residual tile adhesive that may have dried on the surface of the mosaic, using fine abrasive paper (sandpaper). Use a paint-scraper to reach stubborn or awkward areas, such as those next to the wood.

8 Once the residual adhesive is removed, carefully pull off the masking tape from around the edges of the mosaic panels.

9 Finally, remove any remaining dried adhesive from the mosaic panels and polish the surface with a dry, soft cloth.

This traditional design uses the colours seen in ancient Roman mosaics to create a table top suitable for a simple metal base. Unglazed tiles are much easier than glazed tiles to cut and shape for this precise design.

Star Table

You will need

2cm (¾in) thick plywood sheet
String
Drawing pin (thumb tack)
Pencil
Jigsaw (saber saw)
Abrasive paper (sandpaper)
PVA (white) glue
Paintbrushes
Bradawl or awl
Pair of compasses
Pencil
Ruler
Black felt-tipped pen (optional)
Tile nippers
Unglazed ceramic mosaic tiles: white, beige, black and two shades of terracotta
Tile adhesive
Grout spreader
Sponge
Soft cloth

1 To mark a circle on the plywood sheet, tie one end of a length of string, cut to the desired radius of the table top, to a drawing pin (thumb tack), and tie a pencil to the other end. Push the pin into the centre of the plywood, then draw the circle. Cut it out using a jigsaw (saber saw) and sand the edges. Draw your design, adjusting the string to draw concentric circles.

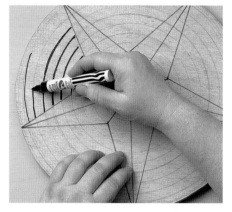

2 Prime one side of the plywood with diluted PVA (white) glue and leave to dry. Score with a bradawl. Using a pair of compasses, draw circles 12mm (½in) apart, working out from the centre, then draw a large star on top. If you wish, go over the design in heavy black felt-tipped pen.

3 Using tile nippers, cut the white tiles into neat quarters. Apply PVA glue to the base in small sections, using a fine paintbrush. Stick the tesserae on to alternate sections of the star. Keep the rows straight and the gaps between the tesserae even and to a minimum. Trim the tesserae as necessary to fit. Continue laying the tesserae until all the white sections are complete.

4 Cut up the beige tiles into neat quarters and fill in the other sections of the star in the same way as the white tiles in step 3.

5 Cut the black tiles into neat quarters and glue around the edge of the plywood. Leave until it is completely dry.

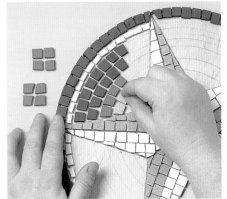

6 Glue a row of black quarter tiles around the outer edge of the table top. Cut some white quarter tiles in half with the mosaic nippers and glue these inside the black circle, keeping the gaps to a minimum. Cut the terracotta tiles into quarters.

7 Using your drawn lines as a guide, fill in the rest of the background with alternating bands of colour. Lay out the tesserae before you glue them in place. Leave to dry overnight. Grout with tile adhesive, then clean the surface with a damp sponge. Leave to dry, then sand off any remaining adhesive and polish with a dry, soft cloth.

This wonderful table is literally strewn with daisies – green stems twine around the legs and a carpet of pretty white flowers spreads over the top. If the table has a rim, saw it off first to make the shape easier to mosaic.

Daisy-covered Table

You will need

Small table

White spirit (paint thinner)

Abrasive paper (sandpaper)

PVA (white) glue

Paintbrush

Bradawl or awl

Soft dark pencil

Thin-glazed ceramic household tiles: yellow, white, green, pale pink

Tile nippers

Tile adhesive

Admix

Flexible knife

Hammer

Piece of sacking (heavy cloth)

Rubber spreader

Sponge

Soft cloth

1 Remove any old wax, dirt, paint or varnish from the table using white spirit (paint thinner), then sand and prime with diluted PVA (white) glue. Leave to dry, then score all the surfaces with a bradawl or awl.

2 Draw flowers and stems twisting around the legs and spreading over the table top. Take care with your design where the legs join the table top.

3 Using tile nippers, cut the yellow tiles into small squares, then nip off the corners to make circles for the centres of the flowers.

4 Cut the white tiles into small, equal size oblongs. Make these into petal shapes by nipping off the corners of each oblong.

▶

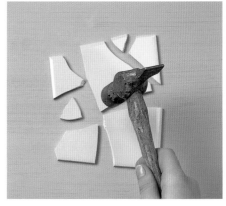

5 Mix the tile adhesive and admix together. Using a flexible knife, spread the mixture over a pencilled flower outline. Press in a yellow flower centre and the white petals – you may need to cut some petals on the legs in half. Complete all the flowers in this way.

6 Spread a thin coat of the adhesive mixture along the pencil outlines of the stems and leaves. Cut the green tiles into appropriate stem and leaf shapes and press them in place. Leave to dry overnight.

7 Using a hammer, break up the pale pink tiles. It is advisable to wrap each tile in a piece of sacking (heavy cloth) to prevent splintering and shattering.

8 Working on a small area at a time, spread the adhesive mixture over the background areas. Press in the pale pink tile pieces to fit. Leave to dry overnight.

9 Grout the mosaic with tile adhesive, using a rubber spreader for the large flat areas and your fingers for the smaller areas. Wipe off the excess adhesive with a damp sponge and leave to dry overnight.

10 Carefully sand the surface of the table top and legs to remove any lumps of dried adhesive still remaining. Wipe with a damp sponge, if necessary, and polish with a dry, soft cloth.

In this project, the mosaics are laid in shapes inset on a surface, rather than over the entire area, and the intervening veneer forms are equally important. The lines give the table a sensual and dynamic feeling.

Stained-glass Table

You will need

110 x 70cm (43 x 28in) MDF (medium-density fiberboard) 18mm (¾in) thick

Soft pencil

Tracing paper

Scissors

Iron

3mm (⅛in) thick oak veneer

Craft (utility) knife

3mm (⅛in) thick stained-glass tiles:
red, iridescent pink and
rippled clear glass

Red chestnut wood stain

Paintbrushes

Clear polyurethane varnish

PVA (white) glue

Contact adhesive

G-clamps

Softwood blocks

Tile grout

Red cement stain

Sponge

Glass cleaner

21mm (⅞in) thick stainless-steel edging to cover edge of MDF and tiles

1 On the piece of MDF (medium-density fiberboard) draw six wavy lines with a soft pencil down the length of the board. These define the three bands that will be filled with the stained-glass and the four bands for the wooden veneer.

2 Trace the lines on to tracing paper. Then cut out templates of the four bands for the veneer. The wooden veneer should be 3mm (⅛in) thick, or the same thickness as the glass tiles to be used for the mosaic, so that they create a flat surface.

3 Iron the cut-out templates flat, using a warm, not hot, heat, as the tracing paper tends to crinkle and fold.

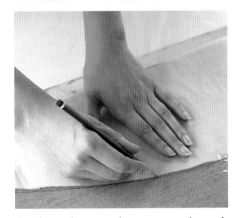

4 Place the templates on to the oak veneer. Using a soft pencil, carefully draw a line around the edge of each template. Placing any straight lines along the straight edge of the veneer makes it easier for cutting.

▶

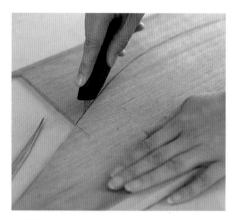

5 With the sharp blade of a craft (utility) knife, and working on a protected surface, score a strong line along the pencil marks. Work the curved lines in sections, removing excess veneer as you go.

6 Place the four cut-out sections of veneer in their correct positions on the table. Using tile nippers, snip the stained-glass tiles into small pieces, laying them in position until the desired effect is achieved. In the planning, be aware of the balance of different coloured and rippled glass.

7 Lay the pieces of veneer on a protected surface and apply two thin coats of red chestnut wood stain. Allow to dry. Apply several coats of clear varnish to each piece, allowing each coat to dry before applying the next.

8 Place the veneer panels back in position on the table. Cover the back of the stained-glass tesserae evenly with PVA (white) glue, using a small paintbrush. Lay the pieces in a random arrangement on the table in a ratio of four red tiles to every two pink and one clear.

9 To stick the veneer down, use contact adhesive, following the manufacturer's instructions carefully. Apply a thin film of this glue on to both the back of the veneer and the surface of the table. After about 10 minutes, or when the glue is tacky, bring the two surfaces together and press down hard, clamp (using softwood blocks to protect the veneer) and leave to dry. Note that once the two surfaces have made contact, no repositioning is possible.

10 Carefully grout the mosaic bands with a grey tile grout mixed with red cement stain. Clean off the excess trying not to get any grout on the veneer. When it is nearly dry, go over the mosaic areas with a sponge dipped in glass cleaner to remove excess grout. When the grout is completely dry, glue the stainless-steel edging in position around the table using contact adhesive.

In this project, the coloured glass tesserae are laid on top of pieces of clear glass. Placing the screen in front of a window by day or a glowing fire at night means that light can shine through it.

Stained-glass Screen

You will need

Mitre block

Tape measure

Hacksaw

3 pieces of 2.5 x 4cm (1 x 1½in) wood, each 206cm (81in) long, with a 12mm (½in) rebate (rabbet)

Wood glue

Hammer

12 corner staples

Dark pencil

Drill

4 small hinges and screws

Screwdriver

Large sheet of paper

Black felt-tipped pen

3 pieces of clear glass, each 70 x 25cm (28 x 10in)

Permanent felt-tipped pen

Glass cutter

7 pieces of coloured glass, 27cm (10½in) square

Clear all-purpose adhesive

Tile grout

Black cement stain

Toothbrush

Paint scraper

Soft cloth

3 pieces of rectangular moulding, each 186cm (74in) long

Panel pins (brads)

12 metal corner plates and screws

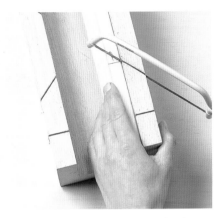

1 Using a mitre block and a hacksaw, cut each piece of rebated (rabbeted) wood into two 74cm (29in) long pieces and two 29cm (11½in) long pieces. These will form the wooden frame for the screen.

2 Lay the pieces of wood out on a flat surface to make three oblong frames. Glue the mitred ends together with wood glue, checking they are at right angles. Leave to dry, then hammer in a corner staple at each corner.

3 Place one frame on top of another, with the rebates facing outwards. With a dark pencil, mark the position of two hinges and their screw holes, as shown. Using a drill, make a shallow guidehole for each screw, then screw in the hinges. Attach the third wooden frame in the same way to form a three-piece screen.

▶

4 Place the three frames face down on a large sheet of paper. Using a black felt-tipped pen, draw around the inner edge of each frame. Then draw a simple design that flows in bands of colour from one frame to the next.

5 Place the pieces of clear glass over the paper drawings – the glass will be slightly larger. Using a permanent felt-tipped pen, trace your design on to the pieces of glass, taking care not to press too hard against them.

6 Using a glass cutter, cut 12 right-angled triangles of coloured glass for the corners of the screen. Reserve them on one side. Cut the rest of the coloured glass into random shaped pieces of roughly similar size.

7 Using clear adhesive, glue the coloured pieces on to the clear glass panels. Work on a section of your design at a time, following each band across to the other panels. Leave to dry for 2 hours.

8 Mix the tile grout with the black cement stain and rub it over the surface of the mosaic. Use a toothbrush to make sure all the gaps are filled. Leave to dry for 1 hour.

9 When completely dry, clean off any smaller areas of excess grout with a soft cloth. Residual, stubborn grout can be carefully removed with a paint scraper.

10 Glue one of the reserved right-angled triangles of coloured glass over the corner of the frames, at the front. Repeat with the other triangles, on each corner of the frame.

11 Cut each length of moulding into two 70cm (28in) lengths and two 23cm (9in) lengths. Place the glass panels within their frames, ensuring that they are the right way up, and slot the beading behind them. Fix them in place with panel pins (brads), being very careful as you use the hammer.

12 Make shallow guideholes with a drill, then screw the corner plates to the back of each corner of the frame. Finally, polish the surface of each of the mosaic panels with a dry, soft cloth.

Walls, floors
and surfaces

Walls in the home are perfect as settings for mosaic. It can cover a whole wall or be used in the form of insets or panels. Mosaic is ideal in hardworking areas such as the hallway, utility room, kitchen or bathroom and is especially suited to floors, being both versatile and durable. If you do not have the time or skill to work a whole floor, an inset panel can be a very effective way of introducing colour and design to your home.

More manageable in size than complete murals, and more realistic projects for someone new to mosaic, decorative splashbacks, wall panels and shelves will brighten any room in the house.

Splashbacks, Panels and Shelves

Since the great strength of mosaic is its impact, an entire wall covered in it may be more than you want. In such cases, the ideal solution is a small area, such as a splashback or decorative panel, or even a shelf, specifically designed to suit its surroundings or its owner, or both.

Splashbacks

Mosaic makes perfect splashbacks for cookers (stoves), kitchen sinks and bathroom basins, transforming such items into something unique to you. The design must be practical, as it will receive much wear and tear. A splashback can be formed of a single panel or tiles grouped together.

In a kitchen, simple checks or plain colours with borders work well, while in a bathroom you might like to suggest the movement of waves and water. If you are aiming for something more personal, here is the opportunity to devise an image that picks up on the room's colour scheme but also incorporates elements that are individual to you and your family, such as your initials, a favourite flower or a family crest.

Friezes

Somewhere between splashbacks and wall panels come friezes. There are occasions when a minimal amount of decoration is all that is needed to

transform an area of the house. A frieze, or similar narrow band or border, may be more effective than a larger element in small spaces such as a downstairs cloakroom or a shower room, or in busy areas such as a porch or hallway, where too much elaboration tends to be overlooked amid the bustle of people coming and going.

A small mosaic could also outline a window (perfect to highlight a porthole-style opening), a fire surround or mantelpiece to great effect.

Above: Watery themes suit mosaic panel splashbacks in kitchens and bathrooms.

Wall panels

A hanging wall panel makes a wonderful picture with depth and impact, and a plainly decorated room can be transformed by a well-executed mosaic panel. Including a border into its design finishes off any mosaic, but if you want to heighten the impression of a work of art, the mosaic panel could be framed before it is hung in position.

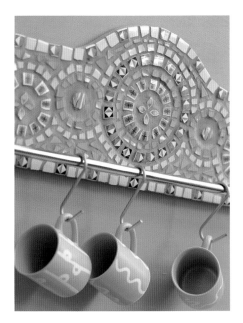

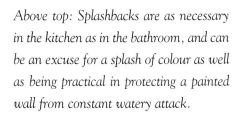

Above top: Splashbacks are as necessary in the kitchen as in the bathroom, and can be an excuse for a splash of colour as well as being practical in protecting a painted wall from constant watery attack.

Above: This useful and colourful decorative kitchen rail is made out of old, broken patterned household china and crockery. The kitchen theme can be carried through by drawing around cups, plates and jars to create the circular designs.

Wall panels can come in all shapes and sizes. A large panel could cover almost an entire wall, dominating the room, while a small one could demand attention by its bold colouring or eye-catching design.

Shelves

A further method of adding mosaic to walls is by way of a shelf or decorated rail. A shelf is an ideal project for a beginner, especially if a simple, all-over design is chosen rather than anything

Above: Gates of the Living – *maximum impact with minimum elaboration in this elegant panel by Elaine M. Goodwin.*

too complicated. Whether the mosaic is bright and colourful, made from pieces of old china, or calm and restful, made from broken slate, the result is still the introduction of a stunning design element into a room in a functional, yet decorative way. The same applies to a mosaiced rack or rail – adding a unique touch of colour.

Hallways, garden rooms, kitchens, utility rooms and bathrooms are obvious choices for mosaic, but it can also furnish living rooms without seeming too cold or hard to walk on.

Interior Flooring

Mosaic is a practical flooring choice for most areas, being versatile and durable – several examples around 2,000 years old are still in very good condition. Most mosaic materials are tough: they resist marks, spills, scuffs and stains, and are not inclined to fade over time. With the right preparation, they will stick to most surfaces and be comfortable under-

foot. Any floor finish must be able to withstand feet, shoes, paws, claws and perhaps wheels as well.

A mosaic, whether covering the whole floor or just part of it, may be all the decoration a floor needs. Ornamentation does not always need to be at eye level to be effective, and treating your room scheme in this way can make a refreshing change.

Above: Mosaic flooring is practical and hard-wearing in a bathroom but must be smooth to protect bare feet.

Left: Children can actually play on this fun and practical mosaic floor. Climb the ladders, but if you land on a snake, you slip back down.

Working on whole floors

There is no reason at all why you should not mosaic a whole floor, but this is a major undertaking, requiring many hours of patient and skilled work. Alternatively, an inset is an effective way of achieving almost the same result with a fraction of the work.

Choose good, hard-wearing materials that are proof against the risk of damage. Stone and suitably glazed clay are ideal; glass is less so but can be used with care. The floor must be level and even before you lay the mosaic, otherwise it never will be.

Right: Classic black and white tiles are enlivened by a floor inset with mosaic in a stylized reptile and ivy leaf design by Elaine M. Goodwin.

Below: Diamonds of stone and rough-textured pebbles would be perfect in a cottage or farmhouse.

It is important to remember scale when designing for floors. The eye will not want so much detail at this distance, either in the design itself or in the size of stone or tesserae: ensure they are not too small, or the overall result will appear too fussy. Large sections of colour with bold elements such as central motifs and borders work well.

This dramatic mosaic creates the invigorating effect of rocks sparkling with drops of water in a mountain stream. This project is quick to complete, as it does not need to be grouted.

Slate Shelf

You will need

2cm (¾in) thick plywood sheet

Saw

Bradawl or awl

PVA (white) glue

Paintbrush

Hammer

Slate

Piece of sacking (heavy cloth)

Tile adhesive

Black cement stain

Flexible knife

Pebbles

Glass globules: blue, grey, white

Silver smalti

Tile nippers

1 Cut the piece of thick plywood to the desired size with a saw. Lightly score one side with a bradawl or awl, then prime with diluted PVA (white) glue.

2 Using a hammer, break the slate into large chunks. It is advisable to wrap the slate in a piece of sacking (heavy cloth) to prevent injury.

3 Mix the tile adhesive with half a teaspoon of black cement stain. Mix to a thick paste with cold water.

4 Using a flexible knife, spread the tile adhesive in a thick, even layer over the scored side of the plywood. Smooth it over the front to conceal the edge.

5 Arrange the broken slate, pebbles, glass globules and silver smalti on a flat surface next to the board in your chosen design, making any adjustments until you are satisfied.

6 Transfer the design, piece by piece, to the board. Tap the slate with the side of the tile nippers to settle it, but do not move any pieces once firmly positioned. Leave to dry overnight.

In this panel, the tiles have been laid very close together to avoid the need for grout. This allows the range of tones used here to relate to one another as directly as possible, giving a luminous, glowing appearance.

Abstract Colour Panel

You will need

Vitreous glass mosaic tiles in various colours

Coloured pencils to match the tiles

Paper

Tracing paper

Tile nippers

MDF (medium-density fiberboard) 50 x 50cm (20 x 20in) with frame

Different coloured felt-tipped pens

Wood stain

Paintbrushes

PVA (white) glue

Soft cloth

1 Match the proposed tile colours to the pencils to enable you to produce an accurate coloured drawing. As this scheme is fairly complex, involving boxes within boxes, and tonal colour changes, a line drawing was produced as a plan for the coloured sketch.

2 Draw an accurate coloured sketch. To get a good idea of how the different blocks of tones and shading will work, put a layer of tracing paper over the line drawing and fill in the coloured areas. Use the tile nippers to cut the mosaic tiles in your chosen colours.

3 Draw the fundamentals of the design on to the board using felt-tipped pens. It is not necessary to mark up any more detail than you see here. The segmented pattern is sketched in black, and the ladder lines in different colours. Stain the frame of the board before starting to stick down the tiles.

4 Sort your tiles into tones of greater or lesser intensity. Paint each area of the board that you are working on with a good layer of PVA (white) glue. If the layer is too thin, the tiles will fail to adhere; if it is too thick, the glue will squeeze between the joints on to the tile face. Start by laying the coloured ladder shapes.

5 Continue working around the board, filling in the different coloured areas as you go. Wipe off any blobs of glue as you work, then wipe over the whole thing with a cloth when you have finished to remove any residual adhesive. Finally, polish with a dry, soft cloth.

Mosaic is an ideal decorative surface or wall cladding for areas in which water is present, such as this splashback for a bathroom basin. It is made from roughly broken tiles, with chips of mirror to catch the light.

Fish Splashback

You will need

Tape measure

4mm (⅛in) thick plywood sheet

Saw

PVA (white) glue

Paintbrush

Soft dark pencil

Bradawl or awl

Ceramic household tiles: light grey, dark grey, soft pink, cream, and soft blue

Hammer

Piece of sacking (heavy cloth)

Tile nippers

Tile adhesive

Flexible knife

Thin edging tiles

Mirror

Soft brush

Plant mister

Drinking straw

Scissors

Abrasive paper (sandpaper)

Soft cloth

Drill

Wall plugs (plastic anchors)

4 domed mirror screws

Screwdriver

1 Measure the width of your basin and cut the plywood to size. Prime the surface with diluted PVA (white) glue. When it is dry, draw a simple fish design on the plywood.

2 Using a bradawl or awl, make a hole through the plywood in each corner.

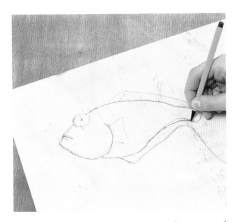

3 Select the colours of the tiles to be used for tesserae; here, two similar greys are used for the fish and a muted pink for the starfish. Smash the tiles into a variety of shapes using the hammer. It is advisable to wrap the tiles in a piece of sacking (heavy cloth) for this procedure.

4 Select a suitable tile that has a soft base with a thin glaze, such as a Mexican tile. Using the tile nippers, nibble two circles for the eyes of the fish. Then use a bradawl or awl to carefully make a hole in the centre of each.

▶

5 Spread some tile adhesive on to the base within the outlines of your drawing. Fix the tesserae within the drawn lines, using a lighter grey for the fins and tail and a darker grey for the body of the fish. Try to find tesserae in shapes that will fit within the drawing and suggest the movement of the fish. Use the pinkish tiles to fill in the starfish outline.

6 When the fish and starfish are complete, smash tiles of the background colour, in this case a soft blue. Spread some tile adhesive on to the base, a small area at a time. Press the background tesserae firmly into the adhesive. Be careful not to tile over the hanging holes in the corners.

7 Cut thin edging tiles into short segments and fix them around the edge of the mosaic. Using tile nippers, cut the mirror into small pieces. Press these tesserae into the larger gaps in the design, on top of a blob of adhesive to keep them level with the other tesserae. Leave to dry for 24 hours.

8 Spoon dry tile adhesive on to the surface of the splashback and brush it into the cracks using a soft brush. Avoid the area around the hanging holes. Spray the surface with plenty of water using a plant mister.

9 Cut a drinking straw into four pieces and stand one over the hole in each corner. Use some tile adhesive to grout around the straws. Leave to dry for 12 hours.

10 Remove the straws and sand off any adhesive remaining on the surface of the splashback, then polish with a dry, soft cloth. Place the splashback against the wall and mark the positions of the screw holes. Drill the holes and insert wall plugs (plastic anchors). Use mirror screws with domed heads to screw the splashback in position.

No artistic skills are required for this stunning mosaic, as the picture is simply an old etching enlarged on a photocopier. The tesserae are glued on to fibreglass mesh, then lowered into position on the floor.

Black-and-white Floor

You will need
Black-and-white image
Clear film (plastic wrap)
Masking tape
Fibreglass mesh
Unglazed ceramic mosaic tiles:
black and white
Tile nippers
PVA (white) glue
Paintbrush
Craft (utility) knife
Tile adhesive
Notched spreader
Flat wooden board
Hammer
Grout spreader
Sponge
Soft cloth

1 Decide on the image you wish to use, or you may wish to build up a picture from various elements. Enlarge on a photocopier to the required size.

2 Working on a large work surface, cover the photocopy with clear film (plastic wrap) and secure the edges with masking tape. If your picture is built up from more than one image, repeat this process for all the sections.

3 Position a piece of fibreglass mesh over the clear film, and tape it down to the work surface with masking tape. Using tile nippers, cut the tiles into quarters.

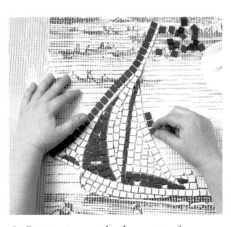

4 Beginning with the main features, such as the boat, glue the tesserae to the fibreglass mesh using PVA (white) glue and a fine paintbrush. Build up the picture, using the light and shade of the photocopy as a guide.

5 Outline the panel with a geometric border in black and white, cutting some of the tesserae in half to make triangular shapes.

6 Fill in the background of the design, simplifying and accentuating the black and white areas, until the photocopy is completely covered. Leave to dry.

7 Using a craft (utility) knife, cut through the mesh and clear film, chopping the mosaic into manageable sections. You may find it helpful to cut around the boat shape, as shown.

8 Turn the sections over and peel off the clear film. Using the craft knife, pierce any holes in the mesh that are clogged with glue.

9 Spread tile adhesive over the bath-room floor, using a notched spreader. Work from the part of the floor furthest away from the door.

10 Carefully lay each section of the mosaic on the tile adhesive, mesh side down.

11 Place a flat wooden board over each part of the mosaic and tap with a hammer to make sure the tesserae are firmly embedded into the adhesive. Leave to dry overnight, then grout with more tile adhesive, using a grout spreader. Wipe away any excess with a damp sponge, then leave to dry. Finally, polish with a dry, soft cloth.

This hearth mosaic has a simple, contemporary feel with a strong use of colour, bringing a new lease of life to this old fireplace. It has been laid using a semi-indirect technique to ensure a smooth finish.

Mosaic Hearth

You will need

Chisel

Hammer

Brown paper

Craft (utility) knife

Scissors

PVA (white) glue

Sponge

Wooden board

Adhesive tape

Pencil

Ruler

Vitreous glass mosaic tiles: dark purple, light purple, and contrasting colours for the border infill

Tile nippers

Matt (flat) cream porcelain tiles

Paintbrush

Tile adhesive

Notched trowel and bucket

Wire (steel) wool

Screwdriver

Tile grout

Abrasive paper (sandpaper)

Soft cloth

1 Using a chisel and hammer, remove any old tiles from the fireplace.

2 Chisel away any remaining tile adhesive. It is essential to have a very smooth surface on which to lay the mosaic if you are to get a good result.

3 To make a template, take a piece of brown paper, larger than the area to be mosaiced, and fold over the edges to fit the space exactly. It can be tricky around the more detailed areas. Using a craft (utility) knife and scissors, cut out the shape accurately. Check it by placing it back into the hearth.

4 Brush away any loose debris from the fireplace. Seal the concrete by sponging some diluted PVA (white) glue all over it. Allow to dry.

5 This technique works in reverse, so turn the template upside down. Place the template on a piece of wooden board and stick it down with adhesive tape to ensure that the paper does not move around.

6 Mark the base line of the border edging at 2mm (¹⁄₁₆in) in from the edge (this allows a margin of error when fitting). Measuring from this line, mark three more lines: one at 2cm (¾in), the second at 7cm (2¾in) and the third at 9cm (3½in). Stick strips of dark purple border tiles with PVA glue along the two narrow bands, paper side down, leaving a 5cm (2in) gap for the detail (see step 7). The bulk of the design is made up of sheets of pale purple vitreous glass, cut with a craft knife and laid in position, paper side down. Fill as much of the space as possible with whole tiles. Clip tiles to fit any gaps left at the back and sides of the mosaic, and stick them in place later.

7 The detail of the border is made from matt (flat) cream porcelain tiles clipped into quarters with the tile nippers. Position these in a central line that runs between and parallel to the two strips of dark purple vitreous glass. Take care that the lines meet neatly at their corners. Then, starting in one corner, make a grid with cut quarters of cream tile at 2.5cm (1in) intervals inside the two dark purple bands. Fill in the gaps with a variety of colours from the vitreous glass range, clipped into quarters. To ensure the correct spacing, lay the tiles down before you stick them in position. Adjust the spacing so that the uniformed design works, taking particular care in the corners.

8 Using a small paintbrush, apply PVA glue to the front of the small tiles, and stick them on to the paper.

9 Apply PVA glue to the paper backing on the light purple tiles and stick them in position on the brown paper, filling in the gaps with the clipped tiles. Leave to dry for several hours. ▶

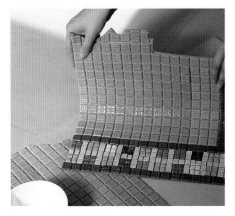

10 Cut up the mosaic into manageable pieces. Lift them up, shaking gently to remove tile fragments and any loose tiles. Stick these back in place.

11 Back on-site, lay the sections of the mosaic, tile-side down. It should fit, and all you will see is brown paper.

12 Lay the sheets carefully to one side, so that the order in which they need to be laid is obvious. Apply some grey tile adhesive to the concrete surface with a notched trowel, ensuring you lay a good even bed. Carefully lay down the sheets, tile-side down. Once you are happy with the positioning of the sheets, press them into the adhesive and rub over the surface with a damp sponge. Leave to dry for 24 hours.

13 Fill a bucket with warm water and dampen the brown paper with a wet sponge. Leave for 5 minutes, then dampen again.

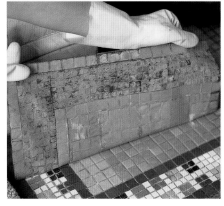

14 When the paper is ready it should peel off easily. Some bits will stick, but these can be cleaned off with wire (steel) wool. Wash the mosaic and glue back any pieces that have come loose.

15 There is a tendency with this technique for adhesive to squeeze up between the gaps, and it tends to be a different colour from the grout. Clear this excess away with a screwdriver.

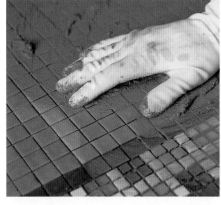

16 Grout the mosaic with a grey tile grout. Remove any excess grout with a damp sponge, then leave it to dry. Sand off any dried-on grout, then polish with a dry, soft cloth.